CW01334565

The Normans

A Captivating Guide to the Norman Conquest and William the Conqueror

© Copyright 2020

All Rights Reserved. No part of this book may be reproduced in any form without permission in writing from the author. Reviewers may quote brief passages in reviews.

Disclaimer: No part of this publication may be reproduced or transmitted in any form or by any means, mechanical or electronic, including photocopying or recording, or by any information storage and retrieval system, or transmitted by email without permission in writing from the publisher.

While all attempts have been made to verify the information provided in this publication, neither the author nor the publisher assumes any responsibility for errors, omissions or contrary interpretations of the subject matter herein.

This book is for entertainment purposes only. The views expressed are those of the author alone, and should not be taken as expert instruction or commands. The reader is responsible for his or her own actions.

Adherence to all applicable laws and regulations, including international, federal, state and local laws governing professional licensing, business practices, advertising and all other aspects of doing business in the US, Canada, UK or any other jurisdiction is the sole responsibility of the purchaser or reader.

Neither the author nor the publisher assumes any responsibility or liability whatsoever on the behalf of the purchaser or reader of these materials. Any perceived slight of any individual or organization is purely unintentional.

Free Bonus from Captivating History (Available for a Limited time)

Hi History Lovers!

Now you have a chance to join our exclusive history list so you can get your first history ebook for free as well as discounts and a potential to get more history books for free! Simply visit the link below to join.

Captivatinghistory.com/ebook

Also, make sure to follow us on Facebook, Twitter and Youtube by searching for Captivating History.

Table of Contents

PART 1: THE NORMAN CONQUEST 1

  INTRODUCTION 2

  CHAPTER 1 - ENGLAND BEFORE THE DEATH OF A PIOUS KING AND THE NORMAN INVASION 5

  CHAPTER 2 - EDWARD THE CONFESSOR AND THE QUESTION OF SUCCESSION 15

  CHAPTER 3 - THE NORWEGIAN KING HARALD HARDRADA 24

  CHAPTER 4 - WILLIAM, DUKE OF NORMANDY 31

  CHAPTER 5 - HAROLD II OF ENGLAND 39

  CHAPTER 6 - VERIFICATION OF EVENTS AND PREPARATIONS FOR WAR 46

  CHAPTER 7 - THE INVASION OF THE NORWEGIAN KING HARALD HARDRADA 53

  CHAPTER 8 - WILLIAM ARRIVES IN ENGLAND 58

  CHAPTER 9 - THE BATTLE OF HASTINGS AND WILLIAM'S CORONATION 65

  CHAPTER 10 - REBELLING AGAINST THE NEW KING AND THE CONSEQUENCES OF DOING SO 74

  CHAPTER 11 - THE DOMESDAY BOOK 85

  CHAPTER 12 - EFFECTS OF THE CONQUEST 90

CHAPTER 13 –RECORDS OF 1066 CE – INSIGHT INTO A TIME OF TURMOIL 100

CONCLUSION 106

PART 2: WILLIAM THE CONQUEROR 109

INTRODUCTION 110

CHAPTER 1 – WILLIAM'S EARLY DAYS: BIRTH, CHILDHOOD, ADOLESCENCE, AND EARLY REIGN OVER THE NORMANS 113

CHAPTER 2 – THE CONQUEST: NORMANDY AND BRITAIN IN THE LATE 10TH CENTURY, THE BATTLE OF HASTINGS, AND THE AFTERMATH 133

CHAPTER 3 – FROM DUKE TO KING: RULING OVER ENGLAND AND NORMANDY 191

CHAPTER 4 – FINAL YEARS AND DEATH 208

CHAPTER 5 – WILLIAM'S CHARACTER: PERSONALITY TRAITS, VIRTUES, FLAWS, AND MOTIVATIONS 211

CONCLUSION 215

HERE'S ANOTHER BOOK BY CAPTIVATING HISTORY THAT YOU MIGHT LIKE 217

FREE BONUS FROM CAPTIVATING HISTORY (AVAILABLE FOR A LIMITED TIME) 218

BIBLIOGRAPHY 219

Part 1: The Norman Conquest

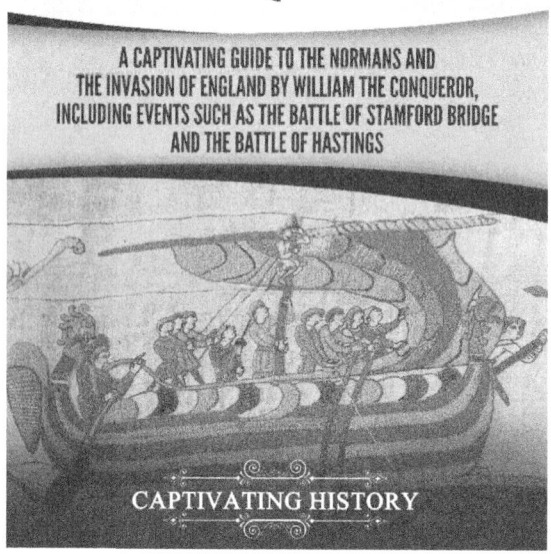

A Captivating Guide to the Normans and the Invasion of England by William the Conqueror, Including Events Such as the Battle of Stamford Bridge and the Battle of Hastings

Introduction

There have been several key events throughout its history that have significantly altered the course of England. The first well-documented shift was when the Romans arrived and took control over the island, but they were hardly the last invaders to alter the path that the nation took. Following the departure of the Romans, the Vikings began to raid England's coasts, and, over time, they began to take control over parts of the island.

After the Romans' departure, the Anglo-Saxons remained in control of the island for several centuries, from 450 to 1066 CE. During this time, Viking leaders would occasionally take control over different parts of the island, but they were largely recorded as pretenders, and after their forcible removal, an Anglo-Saxon would become king again. The legendary King Arthur was based on one of the rulers who defended the island from the invasions of the Vikings.

However, the constant struggles continued well into the 11th century, and in part, they helped to destabilize the Anglo-Saxons. When the Anglo-

Saxon King Æthelred II remarried after the death of his first wife, he chose the daughter of the Duke of Normandy, perhaps in the hopes of establishing some protection from the Vikings. However, his new wife, Emma, was not one to let go once she rose to power. When King Æthelred II died in 1016 and the Vikings again claimed the throne, she married the invader, King Cnut. Had her sons by this king survived, English history could have been even more different than it is today.

Because of the Vikings' successful invasion and Emma's refusal to let her line lose power, one of her sons by King Æthelred II would eventually inherit the throne. King Edward had little interest in ruling, or in anything secular, allowing the Godwinson family to have a lot more control over the kingdom's management than most kings would have allowed. When he died childless in early January 1066, the events of the last couple of decades left a large question over who was the rightful heir. While there was a legitimate heir to the throne (someone who was descended from King Æthelred II and his first wife), he was ignored as three men with less right to the throne fought over who would become king.

The year 1066 CE is one of the largest turning points in British history, with most people today having heard of the Battle of Hastings. The year had begun with the death of Edward the Confessor, a man who would be one of the last Anglo-Saxon kings. In the end, the course of the kingdom's history would shift as William the Bastard became William the Conqueror. He and his people would write their version of the history, meaning much of what we know today should be taken with a healthy dose of skepticism. Much like the "Histories" of Shakespeare are largely propaganda to improve the Tudor claim to the throne, William would ensure that history was recorded in favor of his lineage. Instead of recording events in the form of plays, the history based on William's perspective was recorded in the Bayeux Tapestry, a cloth tapestry that has as many as 75 scenes depicting the Norman invasion. The repercussions of his victory entirely changed the trajectory of the kingdom, as well as that of France.

Chapter 1 – England before the Death of a Pious King and the Norman Invasion

The island of Britain has an incredibly long history with numerous instances of invasions and the departures of those invaders. Each new conquering group of people brought with them the grains of the nation that would eventually form the nation of England. This has made it a nation that not only has a surprisingly diverse range in genetics for an island, but it also has had an effect on nearly every other aspect of England, especially the English language.

In the early days, the Romans were the first known invaders, and much of what is known today about England during that time period is from the Roman perspective. The next major group of invaders was the Vikings, who largely ended up settling down with the people who were already living there. The Vikings were less interested in recording history. While some details are known about the Anglo-Saxon period (with one of the most famous British legends—King Arthur—being from this time), it is not as well documented as one would hope.

The Arrival and Departure of the Romans

Generally noted as the first major conquest of the people of the island, the Romans had marched across continental Europe and decided to continue their conquest beyond the continent. In 43 CE, they conquered the small island off the coast of what would one day be France. It was not the first time that the Romans had traveled across the channel. Julius Caesar had crossed the channel back in 55 BCE, which was met with the approval of the Roman people, although he had no interest in trying to conquer the island or its people.

This changed by 43 CE when Emperor Claudius decided that he wanted to expand the empire that Caesar had started. He sent Aulus Plautius to invade Britain, which the Romans were able to do with little difficulty in the southern parts of the island. But in other parts of the island, the remnants of the British tribes continued to attack the Romans until 51 CE when the Welsh chieftain Caractacus was captured. He was not just a fighter, though, and he befriended many powerful people. When Claudius held a parade to celebrate the victory in Britain, Caractacus was included in the procession. The Romans later recognized him for his courage, and he died in Rome.

Despite the loss of one of Britain's most notable chieftains, the Romans found that the unrest did not end. The leaders of the Celtic people, called the Druids, continued to resist the Romans for much of the Roman occupation. They were largely focused in modern-day Wales, so they did not pose a large threat to the majority of the conquering Roman soldiers. Despite this, there was relative peace for most of the Roman military, who were based on the island for roughly ten years.

When King Prasutagus, who ruled over a British Celtic tribe called the Iceni, died in 60 CE, his wife, Queen Boudica, was not willing to continue the peace. Not only had the Romans stolen their lands, but they had also sexually assaulted her daughters. As the leader of the Iceni, she allied her people with the Trinovantes, another Celtic tribe. Together, they attacked Londinium (modern-day London), Verulamium (modern-day St. Albans), and Camulodunum (modern-day Colchester). All of these Roman posts were burned. When Romans reinforcements returned, the reinforcements nearly wiped out all of her people. To ensure the Romans could not do anything else against her, she quickly committed suicide in either 60 or 61.

The Romans began pressing farther north and west between 70 and 90 CE. By the end of their expansion, they had established positions in Caerleon, Chester, and York. While they had some success against the people in what is now modern-day Scotland, they realized that they were being spread too thin. In 122 CE, Emperor Hadrian commissioned the construction of a large wall that still has remnants along the border with the Scots. When it was finished, Hadrian's Wall stretched for a little over seventy miles going from Newcastle to Carlisle, marking the regions that the Romans considered to be their territory on the island.

Following Hadrian's death in 138 CE, Emperor Antonius Pius decided to push north again with mixed results. He commissioned the construction of a new wall for the territories the Romans did take, naming it Antonine's Wall. By 160 CE, Hadrian's Wall had resumed being the border of the Roman Empire on the island, and the Romans continued to make further attempts to move farther north.

The people in the southern part of the island became accustomed to the Roman settlements. Many of the Roman laws and governmental structures were in place, and as a result, towns began to form in regions that had been more nomadic previously. The modern-day cities of Bath,

Chester, Colchester, Gloucester, Lincoln, St. Albans, and York all have their roots during the Roman occupation. Native peoples could gain power by adopting Roman ways, which helped to establish an aristocracy on the island. The rest of the population saw little change in their daily lives during this time.

The decline of Roman power on the island took roughly 25 years from when it started to when they completely lost control of the nation. Trouble began not on the island but in western continental Europe, where the Germanic tribes were beginning to reclaim their lands from the Romans. The problems were largely internal in Rome as the people in power were increasingly less interested in the betterment of Rome and cared only for their own personal enrichment.

The revolt of Magnus Maximus, the commander of Britain, was the beginning of the decline of Roman control. Roman Emperor Gratian was wildly unpopular, and Maximus saw an opportunity to revolt against the Roman forces in Gaul around 383. He prepared his men in Wales and ensured that enough men were left to fight any potential Irish raiders who saw an opportunity to harm Wales while Maximus and his men were gone. He shuffled men around the island, taking control of the Roman forces for himself.

Ultimately, the way he reorganized the units removed some of the Roman bases, ending Roman rule there. From this point on, Rome did not directly control the island. Instead, it was controlled by men who were usually called usurpers by the Anglo-Saxons. Magnus Maximus left with his men, hoping to take control of the Roman Empire for himself. He failed, and no emperor after that was able to exert the same kind of control over the island.

The erosion of their power was finally seen as the Roman powers were forced off of the island in 409 CE. The Roman way of life began to decline on the island as the people began to reassert their own traditions and laws.

The Anglo-Saxons

The Anglo-Saxons were an established group who inhabited and ruled much of the island by the 5th century. The majority of Britain's population was mostly made up of people from the Germanic tribes of Angles, Jutes, and Saxons, and they had largely made peace with one another and the local inhabitants as they settled on the island. As they were so far from the continent, they were generally left alone during the Anglo-Saxon period, which ran from 410 CE to 1066 CE.

Institutions and regional governments were largely based in the new order that was created once the Romans were gone, and the use of Roman coins largely ceased. The towns that had formed under the Romans were largely abandoned, and the garrisons along Hadrian's Wall became bases for the local military and invaders. Without the Romans, the people were able to return to ruling themselves based on what worked best for their traditions.

By the later part of the 6th century, the Anglo-Saxon society had begun to form based on the people's values, with little influence from the Roman ways that remained in their new societies. Societies formed mainly based on region. Free peasants had control over their lands, and some began to coalesce into their own tribes and eventually kingdoms. Those who were the most successful warriors usually became kings of their small tribes and kingdoms.

One thing that was universal was the adoption of Christianity across the island and in Ireland. Ireland saw a much quicker coalescing of power under the religion. The Irish monk Columba was exiled (some say he exiled himself, while others say he was exiled by those in power) to

Scotland in 565 CE for inciting and participating in violence that led to a civil war. He founded a spiritual movement that stretched well beyond the Emerald Isle and across modern-day Scotland and south into the northern parts of modern-day England. This was a period when knowledge thrived, and people sought more spiritual answers than power. The small kingdoms across both islands saw some struggles, but generally, societies and economies thrived under the more peaceful approach.

The later part of the 8th century and the beginning of the 9th century saw the growth of the Kingdom of Mercia. The political strength and influence that the kingdom had amassed over a couple of hundred years eventually become enviable for its power. Another powerful kingdom in England was also beginning to grow during the 9th century, Wessex. By the end of the century, Wessex was ruled by King Alfred the Great.

The power of these two kingdoms attracted the Norwegians in eastern continental Europe. That was when the Vikings began to raid the English coast.

The Repeated Attacks of the Vikings and the Rise of a Legend

Initially, Alfred did not seem like a candidate for the throne. He was the fifth son of King Æthelwulf of the West Saxons. As the fifth in line to the throne, he was largely left to pursue his own interests, which mostly revolved around learning and acquiring knowledge. This probably caused him to be less interested in becoming king, as being one would have limited how much time he could use to study and learn. Ironically, this is likely what made him such a great leader. The knowledge that he accumulated during his early years was probably the reason why he was able to accomplish so much, enough to be the basis for the legendary King Arthur. He was certainly one of the most notable rulers on the island.

As the son of a king, military strategy was certainly something he would be expected to know, even if he was not considered as a serious contender for the throne. By 868 CE, he was in active service in the military and joined King Æthelred I (his brother) in assisting King Burgred of Mercia against the Danish invasion. The Danes had arrived in East Anglia around 865 CE, and by 867 CE, they were in control of Northumbria. However, the Danish refused to fight, and a peace was negotiated. In 871 CE, the Danes again began to expand their grasp over the island, attacking Wessex. Alfred again joined his brother, and they engaged in several battles against the Danish forces. When Æthelred died that same year, Alfred was the next in line for the throne. However, he did not find success in his first battle against the Danes as the new king. The peace that followed the battle of Wilton did give the Danish invaders time to pause and consider their options. While the Danes had not failed in the battle, the West Saxon forces proved to offer more resistance than the Danes had anticipated. For the next five years, the Danish held off instigating any more battles against the new king.

In 876 CE, the Danes resumed their assault on the southwestern part of modern-day England. In 877 CE, they pulled back because they had accomplished very little with their skirmishes over roughly a year. Perhaps the five years that they had refrained from attacking Alfred and his military made them underestimate their opponent. It is also possible that during that time Alfred had spent more time ensuring that the military was ready for battle. Because the Danes had been so problematic throughout his entire life, there is little doubt that Alfred knew that they would try again to expand into his kingdom.

A third explanation could be that they wanted to gain the element of surprise. 878 CE had barely started when they attacked Wessex once more. During that initial push, they were able to take control of

Chippenham, resulting in the majority of Alfred's forces relenting. It was said that all of the West Saxons submitted to the Danes with the exception of their king. Over the course of the next few weeks, he reminded the Danes of his presence through guerilla warfare. As he hounded the Danish with these random attacks, he also managed to assemble enough men to have a new army to support him less than two months after Easter. With his men, King Alfred defeated the Danes at the Battle of Edington. Following their surrender, the Danish king, Guthrum, agreed to be baptized into the Christian religion.

Following this last defeat of the Danes, Alfred was free to control the other aspects of his kingdom until 885 CE. It was at this point that the East Anglian Danes began to attack his kingdom. It took him a year, but in 886 CE, Alfred turned the tide and went on the offensive against this newest threat. When he was able to take what is now modern-day London, all of the English people who were not residing in Danish-held lands chose to acknowledge Alfred as their rightful king. Alfred may not have continued to press the Danish, but his son, Edward the Elder, was able to use the leverage that Alfred had gained by taking London to push farther into the Danish territories after he became king.

One of the primary reasons that Alfred did not continue to stretch his kingdom across the southern part of the island was because the Danish began to plan invasions from the continent. The new round of invasions lasted from 892 to 896 CE, in which Alfred proved that his successes in warfare were not a fluke. His ability to take defensive positions made it incredibly difficult for the Danish to gain any new ground. Any time Alfred had any available resources, he had old structures (particularly forts) strengthened, and then new ones were built in more strategic areas. He ensured that England's defensive posts were perpetually manned, leaving little chance for the Danes to launch a successful surprise attack.

He started having his own ships built in 875 CE, so when new waves of invaders came, he was able to meet them and drive them back to the continent.

Nor was a secure defense his only military strength. Alfred understood that he needed the help of the other island kings, and he maintained a positive relationship with the rulers of Mercia and Wales. When they required assistance, he provided them with support, and they reciprocated when his people were under attack.

Beyond the Fighting

While he is famous for his military prowess, Alfred the Great was a capable leader in many other ways. As his interest lay more in traditional education and literature, he learned how to govern based on what other great rulers before him had done. He used the example of rulers like Charlemagne to restructure the different systems in the kingdom, such as the financial and justice systems, making them more efficient.

He was also intent on making sure that those in power did not exploit or oppress the weak or lower-class peoples of his kingdom. The practice of feuding, the practice of resolving a dispute between parties or families through a private war, was restricted (it could not be entirely banned as it was a part of the culture).

However, it was his reverence for learning that really set Alfred apart from other leaders. He believed that the Viking raids were a sign from the Christian god that people needed to repent for their sins. As long as they sinned, the Vikings would continue to attack. However, the lack of learning was part of the root cause of the problems, including the sins of the people. During the period of peace between 878 and 885 CE, he had scholars join him at court so that they could impart more knowledge and instruct him and others in Latin. He required all freemen who had time to learn to read English so that they could read the books that would give them useful and religious knowledge. Latin was largely only known among those in the Church. Alfred wanted his people to be able to read, so it made more sense for them to speak in their native tongue than to try to learn to read a language that they were largely only exposed to during religious ceremonies.

Although he was a very capable military leader, it was the changes that he made within the empire itself while keeping his people safe from repeated attacks that earned Alfred the epithet "the Great." More than just a knowledgeable military strategist, he was a humanitarian and sought to improve the lives of the people across England. He was remembered for centuries as the ideal king.

It is the society that he had established by the time of his death that had prepared the island for peace and prosperity. Smaller regions and principalities had been absorbed under him, and his kingdom was allied with the large kingdoms around them. The societies that grew out of his religious bent spread across most of Britain. It is the world as influenced by King Alfred that is generally considered the society of the Anglo-Saxons, and he remains one of the most renowned leaders, not only of their golden age but for all of British history.

Chapter 2 – Edward the Confessor and the Question of Succession

By the year 1066, England was a very different place than it had been at the beginning of the Anglo-Saxon period. However, that way of life was about to change significantly, and a new era was about to start on the island. This new period was initiated by another departure, but instead of removing a group of invaders, the people were about to experience a significant shift because of the death of their king.

King Edward the Confessor had lived a largely pious life, after having lived a very tumultuous life during his childhood and early adulthood. Given what had happened to him, it might have been expected that he would be more aware of how much trouble the nation could face if the king did not have an heir. Despite everything that he went through, though, Edward never had any children, largely owing to the tense relationship he had with his wife and her family.

When he died without any children, his kingdom faced one of the greatest problems it had seen since King Alfred's constant struggles against the Vikings. Unlike the earlier years of the Anglo-Saxon era, the kingdom was much larger, and the king was considerably more powerful than even King Alfred had been. Because of Edward's desire to focus on his spiritual life, England became engulfed in a civil war that changed the direction of the kingdom's future.

Edward's Life

Edward's desire to focus on the spiritual is understandable. Although he was the son of King Æthelred II and his wife, Emma of Normandy (the daughter of Richard I of Normandy), there was no guarantee that he would take the throne after his father's death. Edward's legitimate claim to the throne was threatened by the constant invasions by the Danes in 1013 CE, which caused the royal family to flee England and move to Normandy. Naturally, their apparent cowardice did not gain them friends among the English, and the English people were forced to face the invaders without their king.

The royal family took up residence in Normandy (part of modern-day northern France), where they lived in exile for a year. During this time, they planned how they would return to their kingdom and place their family in power once more. Edward accompanied several diplomats to England, where they negotiated the return of Æthelred II as king. This apparent good fortune did not last long as the newly restored king died in 1016.

Edmund Ironside would rule after Æthelred II's death from April until November 1016. During his incredibly short reign, he managed to put up a strong resistance to the Vikings led by King Cnut. His place in the line of succession was questionable as more support was given to the Viking king. Unfortunately for Edmund Ironside and those of Anglo-Saxon descent, he died soon after taking the throne. The cause of his death is not certain, but it is postured that he died of natural causes.

This unfortunate turn of events for the royal family was an opportunity for the Danes, who again returned to invade the island. Without the king and the kind of support they needed, the queen and Edward returned to a life of exile in Normandy for several decades.

However, Queen Emma was not content to remain in exile. With her husband dead, she had a unique opportunity to give the invading Danish a legitimacy that they lacked to claim the throne—she could marry their king, Cnut. Together, they had another son and a daughter, who would one day become the queen of the German territories.

Naturally, the desertion of his mother did not sit well with the future king. Edward seemed to retain resentment against his mother for most of his life, although some historians have argued that she did the best she could under the circumstances. The children of King Æthelred II continued to live in exile while their mother lived with her new husband and their growing family in England. Edward did not marry while he was in exile, choosing to spend more time hunting and acting like a nobleman than in looking for a resolution of the problem against his mother and her new family. His life was largely mundane until 1035, which was when his stepfather, Cnut, died.

At the time of Cnut's death in England, his son with Emma, Harthacnut, was occupied with conducting a war against Magnus I of Norway. Cnut had collected a number of lands during his time as king, including England, Denmark, Norway, and some of Sweden, lands that his son was trying to maintain within a single kingdom—a task that he failed to achieve. With the king dead and the prince (who became king of Denmark after his father's death) abroad fighting another war, Emma was forced to face the reality that the son she had doted on was not likely to get the throne because the British people preferred her stepson, Harold

Harefoot, who was the son of Cnut. Faced with the possibility of her lineage being removed from the throne, Emma finally turned to the children whom she had left in exile when she returned to power in England. Both Edward and his brother, Alfred Ætheling, returned to England. They both became entangled in battles, and Harold Harefoot captured and killed Alfred in 1036.

Emma waited for her son Harthacnut to return to her so that they could remove Harold from power. Having escaped from England after his return there, Edward claimed to have no interest in the throne. That left Harthacnut as Emma's only way of carrying on her family's line as the rulers of the kingdom.

Harthacnut was working to create a larger fleet (he only had ten ships when he landed in Flanders in 1039), but before he had a chance to attack his half-brother, Harold died in early 1040. Emma and Harthacnut returned to England to reclaim the throne that they had a better claim over the last remaining son of the late King Æthelred II. Cnut was seen as a usurper, and Emma was only queen through marriage, not by blood. Though Harthacnut was Emma's favorite child, both he and the queen extended an invitation for Edward to join them in England, where he would rule as a joint king.

Edward's claim to the throne was actually stronger, as he was the only living son of King Æthelred II, but he had spent most of his life living abroad. Despite having said he was not interested in ruling, Edward did return and worked alongside his half-brother to rule the kingdom. In 1042, Edward found himself in a completely different situation following the death of Harthacnut. Just like Harold, Harthacnut did not have any children, leaving the nation in turmoil as people tried to decide who would next sit on the throne. Harthacnut had a cousin named Sweyn Estridsson who considered himself to be the rightful heir, and there were others who were mentioned as being potential kings, such as Magnus I of Norway—the man that Harthacnut had been fighting when his father died and the man that became king of Denmark when Harthacnut died. Rumors said that Emma had considered Magnus, but ultimately, she supported Edward.

By this time, Edward, who was 39 years old, was already older than most Anglo-Saxon kings had been when they died. Edward went on to give England more than two decades of stable rule, and the nation prospered as a result. The early years of his reign were tumultuous as some claimants felt they had a better right to the throne, and he was largely a stranger to everyone in England, after having spent about a quarter of a century living in exile. His biggest opponent was the one who had initially supported him—his mother, Emma.

Despite the fact that Edward had a better claim to the throne than most other possible candidates, Emma (who had a long history of scheming against the kings with Godwin, Earl of Wessex) plotted against her son, in part because she wanted to retain control of England as queen. Her frequent co-conspirator, Godwin, retained considerable power and ruled in all but name for eleven years. Edward appeared to be content with the arrangement in the beginning, having spent much of his life far from London. Godwin had the support of the people, and Edward was aware that he was not as popular or commanding as the man who had lived in England through decades of unrest.

In 1045, Edward married Godwin's daughter, Edith, to give the powerful man a blood relation closer to the throne. However, the king and the shadow king did not always agree on issues and resolutions. In 1049, they had irreconcilable differences, and Edward began to take a larger role in the governing of the realm. Two years later, he declared the Godwin family outlaws, including his own wife. Unfortunately, for the king, his reliance on and favoritism shown to foreigners quickly lost him the goodwill of the people. When Godwin returned in 1052 with his sons and an army, the English people were willing to support him. Edward retained his position as king, but he had to take his wife back and restore all of the Godwin lands to the family.

The following year, 1053, Godwin died, and his son, Harold Godwinson, began to take the place of his father, particularly when it came to keeping the approval of the people. There was one way that Edward could keep his brother-in-law in line, and that was through dangling the throne as a potential option. As Edward had no heirs and had no inclination to have them, it was a tactic that he successfully used for over two decades to keep people loyal to him.

Promises about Succession

For years, it is said that Edward held the promise of the line of succession out to people to get what he wanted or needed, but Harold was essentially a shadow king after his father died. With no clear successor to the throne, it certainly was a very powerful bargaining chip for a man who was not popular with the people he ruled. Queen Elizabeth I would do something similar several centuries later when she became queen and was still unmarried (the primary difference being that she was incredibly popular with the people).

Harold proved that he was a capable leader, even before Edward died, as he finally forced Wales to submit to English rule and also negotiated a peace with the Northumbrians. All of this he did between 1063 and 1065. However, he managed to ostracize his brother, Tostig, who would later side against him when the Vikings invaded.

Despite his strength as a leader, the person with a claim to the throne through actual blood relations was William, the Duke of Normandy, more commonly known in history as William the Conqueror. As Edward's distant cousin, he had a much stronger claim to the throne in terms of blood, and some historians believe that Edward actually promised the throne to William. Though Harold was popular with the people, he was not a blood relation to the royal family, and there was no chance that his sister would ever make the connection valid. Edward had taken her back as his wife because he had been forced to; that did not mean that he felt compelled to further his own line. With the capable William as a potential successor, Edward likely felt that the best solution was to pass the throne on to someone who was capable and had already been through similar hardships as himself. Or perhaps he felt that this was the best way to get back at the family who had forced so much on him after trying to remove him from the throne, attempts that were backed by his own mother.

However, it is also possible that he chose Harold as the next king because Edward knew that Harold had the support of the people. Essentially, the Godwin family had been ruling the country in all but name since Edward had been restored to the throne. Harold was not only popular; he had grown up in the country and had much stronger ties to England than William. Having been unpopular because he had spent much of his life in exile and was not familiar with the customs or traditions like the Godwin family, it is possible that Edward actually did believe that Harold was the best suited to rule the people. William had not lived in the country, which made him less likely to take the best interests of the people in mind. He also had gained a reputation for being brutal and merciless, two things that Edward the Confessor would almost certainly have detested in a leader. The Godwins may have given Edward problems, but they had also allowed the king to be largely left to his own devices, focusing on the spiritual instead of the day-to-day workings of the kingdom. And the country had prospered because of it.

Considering how poorly his mother had treated him over the course of his life, it is difficult to blame Edward for not having children, but he definitely should have made it clear who was to take the throne when he died. Instead, people were left to believe the words of those who had been with him in his final moments.

Edward's Death and the Island on Edge

When he was dying, Edward finally gave his decision as to who he wanted as his successor. According to those who had been with him as he was dying, the king named Harold to be his successor. After everything that had happened during his life, Edward should have known how much people would contest anything that was said from his deathbed. For someone who was said to be pious, Edward had to be aware that his years of dangling the succession in front of others was going to cause infighting because all of these people had been led to believe that they had a chance of being king. That does not even account for the people who felt they had a claim once the childless king died.

Edward's childless marriage later came to be seen as a sign of just how pious he was, earning him sainthood and the name Edward the Confessor. Naturally, this overlooks the problems that his childlessness actually did cause for England. The fact that he didn't have children also was not likely a result of his piousness, though it is not certain why he didn't have children. It could have been a disinterest in having a family after what he had experienced, or he simply didn't want another distraction from what he felt was important. In contrast to those who feel his life mirrored his angelic nature, some believe he was an ineffective ruler, while others believe that he was shrewd and knew his own limitations. As king, the only power that he insisted on retaining was in naming the bishops of the Church; most of the other powers of his position were exercised by Godwin and his son for most of Edward's reign. Although he had accepted the throne, Edward proved that he had not been entirely untruthful when he said he did not want it. His only real interest was in ensuring that the Church had the support that it needed.

This is why it is possible that he actually did leave the kingdom to Harold. Even though Edward had not wanted to have the Godwin family restored to power, they were placed back in power in all but name anyway. Godwin and his son did all of the things that Edward did not want to do, as he did not feel that those roles were important. While he was pushing to have a better, more enlightened Church, the Godwins helped the nation to prosper, creating a stable life for the people of England.

When Edward died, he left a power vacuum that would not be resolved peacefully. The new king, Harold Godwinson, reigning as Harold II, was crowned the next day, but that did not resolve the question of who the rightful heir to the throne was. Edward had all but ensured that the question of succession would only be settled through war.

When Edward died on January 5th, 1066, it was just a matter of time before those who felt that they had a claim to the throne came forward, shattering the security that the kingdom had known under Edward and the shadow king Harold. Though there is definitely a lot of doubt cast on who he left the throne to, it is not likely that Edward actually left it to William. Harold and his wife were already at hand, whereas William resided in Normandy, across the English Channel. Harold knew the inner workings of being king since he had been doing it for years. Logically, Harold made the most sense. While it meant the kingdom would be passing out of the hands of his lineage, Edward could have been ensuring that the nation continued to be ruled by an Anglo-Saxon. William was decidedly not one of them, and with his reputation, it is difficult to imagine Edward actually naming him as the kingdom's successor. Or perhaps Edward was largely indifferent because he did not care for the position himself.

Chapter 3 – The Norwegian King Harald Hardrada

There were a number of people who sought to follow Edward the Confessor as the English king, but none of them had quite the blood claim that William of Normandy had. The majority of those who wanted to rule the island only had claims based on the usurpers who had taken it from the native people.

The man who had been given the crown, Harold Godwinson, was not only a member of the English nobility, but he also had a lot of support from the people of England. He and his father had long held considerable power, and he was favored over many of the people who had decided to try to lay a claim to the throne. The fact that he was not related by blood was not seen as a problem by many of the Anglo-Saxons. King Harald, on the other hand, had no claim based on blood or right of succession. His interest was largely in expanding to the island that had prospered so well under the Godwin family.

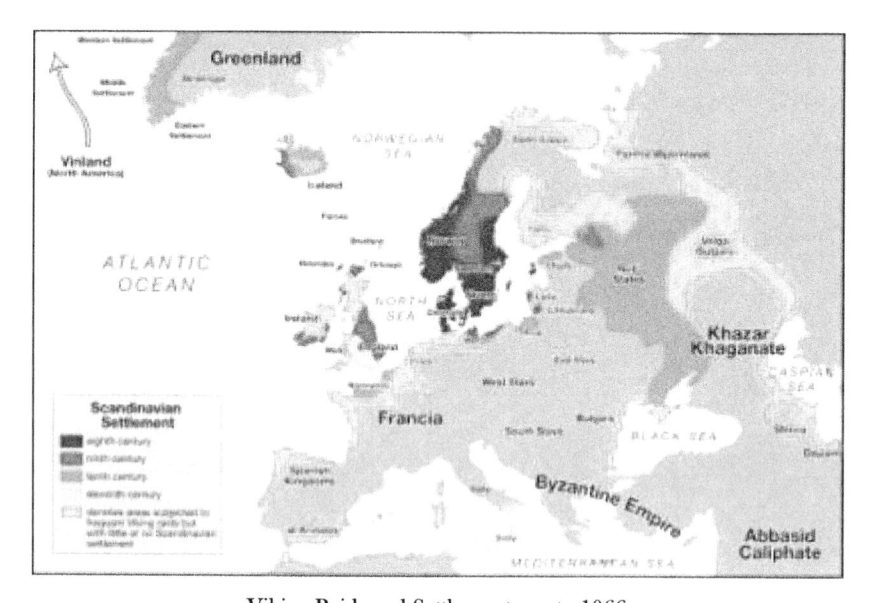

Viking Raids and Settlements up to 1066
https://commons.wikimedia.org/wiki/File:Viking_Expansion.svg

King Harald Hardrada's Life before Invading England

Harald Sigurdsson, who later earned the well-known epithet "Hardrada," meaning hard ruler, was the son of one of the major Norwegian chieftains, a renowned Viking named Sigurd Syr. The family claimed to have been descended from the first king of Norway named Harald Fairhair, although the claim may have been made following Hardrada's death so that his actions would be considered legitimate. Olaf, his half-brother, had been chosen by five minor chieftains to be the king of Norway.

When King Cnut took the throne of Denmark in 1029 CE, Olaf and Harald resisted. The disputes between the families resulted in Olaf being exiled, but he did not stay away for long. In 1030, Olaf returned to Norway, and he and his forces were planning to remove Cnut from his position as king. Harald was staunchly on Olaf's side, and they fought Cnut in the Battle of Stiklestad, where Olaf was killed. Only sixteen years old during that battle, Harald was largely untested as a warrior. He made it out of the battle with his life, but he sustained injuries and was exiled for his participation in the insurrection against the king.

He spent many of the succeeding years in exile, during which time he gained the military experience he needed to try to remove the king again. He spent time in part of modern-day Russia and gained the necessary battle experience against adversaries who were less organized than the men under King Cnut. Harald made a name for himself as a capable warrior, and he was able to attract a band of a few hundred men to fight under him.

With his experienced men, Harald went to the capital of the Byzantine Empire, Constantinople, in roughly 1034. Although they were Vikings, important people of the empire took notice of them, and they were soon hired to be a part of the renowned Varangian Guard. The primary responsibility of the Varangian Guard was to protect the emperor. During his time working as a member of the elite fighters, Harald traveled into much of the world that would have been considered exotic where he came from, such as modern-day Iraq. They went with the negotiators from the Byzantine Empire to Jerusalem, as well as fighting against a range of other enemies on the Mediterranean Sea. This gave him the experience he needed in fighting on water and having to plan for other, less familiar methods of fighting.

By 1041, the politics of the empire had changed, and the Byzantine emperor that Harald and his men had served was dead. As Michael V and Empress Zoë vied for power, Harald went out of favor, perhaps because he supported the former empress, even after Michael V had been given control over the empire. Harald was subsequently imprisoned, though the reason for it has been obscured. Several reasons have come down over the centuries, including an accusation of defrauding the emperor, murder, and defiling a noblewoman. Given the large differences in potential reasons, it is most likely that Michael V and his allies were simply looking to neutralize Harald. The prison could not contain him, though, and upon his escape, Harald rejoined the Varangian Guard to fight against the new emperor. They were successful, and Michael V was removed from power.

It did not take a year before he was again out of favor with Empress Zoë. Realizing that his time in Constantinople was up, he left before he could again be accused of further crimes. However, Empress Zoë rejected his request to leave the Varangian Guard. Harald did not stick around, slipping out of the Byzantine Empire with those men who chose to leave with him. They took control of two ships, losing one to the iron chains in the strait (an obstacle placed across navigable waters to prevent ships from using the waters). After his time fighting the Muslims and other enemies of the empire, Harald knew how the Byzantines would try to catch him, and a mixture of luck and skill helped him escape and finally return to Kievan Rus' in 1042.

During his time away from his people, Harald had accumulated a lot of wealth, most of which he brought with him. Over time, he had sent the wealth that he gathered to the Grand Prince Yaroslav I (known as Yaroslav the Wise), the leader of the people Harald had helped after the death of Olaf, for safekeeping. Having once failed to woo the leader's daughter, Harald was successful the second time around. Yaroslav allowed the marriage, despite Harald's lack of title or claims to the Kievan Rus' throne.

Deciding it was time to return to his native lands of Norway, Harald packed up his riches and new wife and went to try to reclaim the throne. Upon his arrival, he found the royalty to be totally different than when he had left. King Cnut had died in England, and his eldest sons had likewise perished during Harald's absence. The bastard son of his half-brother

Olaf, Magnus I, or Magnus the Good, had ascended to the throne, putting the lands back in his family's bloodline. Despite having supported Olaf, in 1046, Harald decided to challenge his nephew for the throne. To bolster his forces, he allied with Anund Jacob, the king of Sweden, who also felt that he had the right to take the Norwegian throne. They also allied with Sweyn Estridsson, Harthacnut's cousin, who had a much lesser claim to the throne.

Together, the three leaders raided all along the Danish coast, harassing Magnus with the traditional lightning-quick strikes for which the Vikings are still infamous. Seeing that this was not only harming his people but also making him less popular, Magnus' advisors pushed for the king of Norway and Denmark to split control with the battle-hardened Harald. His uncle would be allowed to take the throne of Norway, ruling the people under Magnus, who would retain the throne of Denmark. Harald would have to agree to Magnus being the overlord of the two countries, but he would be allowed to largely manage Norway as he saw fit. Harald agreed, and the two established their own courts and power within their respective countries, rarely meeting to discuss the affairs of their nations.

This arrangement did not last long as Magnus died in 1047, and he had no sons (legitimate or illegitimate) to rule after him. He had not wanted Harald to succeed him, so before his death, Magnus the Good named Sweyn Estridsson to be his successor. This was certainly ironic as Magnus had beaten Sweyn while Harald was off fighting for the empire, and Sweyn had allied with Harald against Magnus upon Harald's return to the region.

How prepared Sweyn was for the inevitable attack by Harald is unclear, but Harald definitely made the first move to try to restore the two kingdoms under one ruler. Instead of invading Denmark in a major assault, Harald opted to use the same tactics he and Sweyn had used against Magnus. The lightning raids along the Danish coast proved to be far less effective as Sweyn did not budge when the same tactics were used against him.

This struggle to combine the two nations under one king resulted in fifteen years of war, and the two leaders were finally forced to face off at the Battle of Niså in early August 1062. With the knowledge of far more diverse and foreign attacks at his disposal (thanks to his time working for the empire), Harald emerged victorious, though it did not accomplish what he had wanted. Sweyn fled the battle with many of his close advisors and most trusted men. Sweyn did not have the military prowess that Harald had, but he also knew that and had no problem fleeing when the odds were stacked against him. Harald and Sweyn continued to fight for another three years before Harald finally opted for peace. In 1065, Harald finally made a truce with the Danish king.

By this time, Harald was fifty years old. Having started fighting for control of Norway when he was just sixteen years old, fighting was one of the things that Harald understood best. With a truce in place with Sweyn, the Norwegian king became restless and decided to turn his attentions elsewhere. The obvious target for his attention was the riches of Britain, a land that the Vikings had targeted for roughly the last two and a half centuries. If he could bring England into his realm, as King Cnut had done, Harald felt that he would finally have a large kingdom to control and a way to ensure that his name went down in history.

King Harald's Claim to the Throne

Of all those laying claim to be the next king of England, King Harald had the weakest claim, even according to the Viking rules. King Cnut had ruled all of Denmark and Norway before taking on England. The line of succession would have meant that the ruler of all the continental kingdoms would also rule England, something that Harald had failed to achieve. The kingdom was fractured in large part because of Harald.

More importantly, the Anglo-Saxons did not recognize King Cnut as a legitimate king. To them, he had been a pretender. There was no point where they would have wanted another Viking on the throne, so even if King Harald had successfully taken the continental part of the old kingdom back, he would not have been recognized as legitimate to the people of the island.

Chapter 4 – William, Duke of Normandy

Before he became known as William the Conqueror, the man who would one day be the king of England was known as William the Bastard. This was both an identification of the situation of his birth and the reputation he had gained over the years as he grew up in Normandy. It is also possibly true that because of his illegitimate status, he felt that he had to prove himself and be tougher than the legitimate sons of Robert I. However, his desire for power was typically on full display as William eventually began to threaten the French king, Henry I. His distant kinship to Edward the Confessor (a first cousin once removed) and a claim that Harold Godwinson had promised to support him (several years before Edward's death) would be his primary reasons for seeking to bring England under his control.

Robert I of Normandy

William was born to Duke Robert I of Normandy and Herleva, his mistress, who was better known as Arletta. While William's father was a member of the nobility, his mother was just the daughter of a tanner with no noble blood. William's maternal grandfather was a successful merchant who had accumulated enough wealth to attract the attention of the members of the nobility. Herleva and Duke Robert I of Normandy did not stay together, and she would eventually marry Herluin de Conteville and have two sons with her husband, giving William two half-siblings.

William's father, Duke Robert I of Normandy, was known by two names: Robert le Magnifique (Robert the Magnificent) to his friends and family, and Robert le Diable (Robert the Devil) to his enemies. He also had a claim to the English throne as he was the great-grandson of Richard I of Normandy (father to Emma, Edward's mother). Upon his father's death, Robert fought with his brother, Richard III of Normandy, about who would control Normandy. Richard III was the elder son, which gave him a better claim to take over the region. However, Richard III died not too long after taking control, and upon his death, Robert I took over the rule of Normandy. With Normandy finally under his control, Robert quickly decided that it was not enough.

Robert I proved to be a fairly demanding ruler and a horrible neighbor, as he claimed lands from various fiefdoms around him and from the Church. He bullied lesser aristocrats, taking their lands and demanding their allegiance. All of this meant that after his brother's death, Robert I had more influence than when he had initially contested Richard III's claim to the throne. Soon, Robert II of France, also known as Robert the Pious, died in 1031. Robert I had been living in Normandy, and with his large power base, he decided to back Henry I of France for the throne. Robert I of Normandy died without any legitimate heirs in 1035 CE.

William's Early Life

Born in 1027 or 1028, William's illegitimacy was not as detrimental to his status as it was to families with less status or wealth; however, it should have excluded him as the heir to Normandy. With wealth on one side and power on the other, he was always going to have a fairly easy time in life, even if he should not have been able to take over his father's lands. William had two half-brothers, Odo of Bayeux (who became the bishop of Bayeux) and Robert, Count of Mortain (who became the earl of Kent), after his mother married. They would prove to be very helpful to him as they always supported him in his endeavors.

After Robert I of Normandy died while on a pilgrimage to Jerusalem, the wheels of the plans he had put in place to ensure his bloodline continued were tested. Knowing that he had no other heirs, Robert I had taken some steps to ensure that his lineage would continue to rule after his death. To guarantee that his lineage would be recognized through his illegitimate son, he had his barons take an oath of loyalty to William. The problem was that without Robert I around, there was no guarantee that his wishes would be respected (a problem that his line would later face in England).

With so much power having been accumulated during Robert I's reign, the people needed someone to take control and help the region to prosper as quickly as possible. Though he was an illegitimate son, William was the most obvious choice. Despite the circumstances of his birth, the nobles honored their oaths to support William as the new duke, and he was quickly recognized as the next successor to the dukedom. It did mean ignoring the rules since a child born out of wedlock meant that a person could never inherit or lay claim to any power that their parents had.

The major problem, though, was that he was only around seven years old. For the next two years, the Duchy of Normandy was managed by William's great uncle, Gilbert, Count of Brionne. The problems of the region were already beginning to simmer, though, and without the tough Duke Robert I in control, the nobles began to rebel. This resulted in a civil war within Normandy, and Gilbert was killed. Though he was still young, William did have a number of powerful relatives and supporters, such as the archbishop of Rouen, who was his uncle Mauger, and Herluin de Conteville (his stepfather). Henry I of France helped him to put down the dukes trying to cut into his territories because the civil war was threatening to damage trade in France, as one of the main trade routes ran through Normandy.

When William turned fifteen years old, the French king, Henry I, knighted him. From that point on, William was largely on his own to take care of Normandy, though he did have help when he needed it. However, King Henry I did not remain as one of his allies. In 1047, problems related to William's rising power finally became more apparent as regions around Normandy had become unstable. Seeing such a young child on the throne had made those around Normandy decide that it was now the time to start trying to chip away at the powerful dukedom. It is clear why William developed such a hardline against others as he had been fighting to keep his dukedom intact since he was a young child. He saw some of his relatives killed as they tried to aid him, and some of his former supporters turned on him. After he finally ended the rebellions, William began to seek to expand his own empire. For twenty years, he demonstrated that the circumstances of his youth had proven to be highly effective in teaching him how to best strategize against his enemies. He became so efficient at consolidating his power that he disrupted the power balance in France.

To this day, he is known as one of the most formidable strategists and military commanders of the Middle Ages. Most people today have heard one or both of his names (William the Bastard and William the Conqueror), even if they are not entirely sure who he is or why he is still known today. His reputation began long before he reached the shores of England because of the turmoil that he experienced at such a young age.

Rebellions within the region were problematic, but King Henry I of France also turned against him in 1054 and attacked William. Over time, William had terrorized and bullied people into ensuring things went his way. Frequently attacking Flanders and Anjou, William became one of the most powerful men in France, making Henry I very uncomfortable. King Henry I feared the unrivaled power William had gained by upsetting or intimidating the majority of France, as he had either taken control of many different regions or strategically had marriages arranged between his nobles and his rivals. Ultimately, he became the most powerful man in France.

William not only put down the rebellions within Normandy, but he and his forces also defeated King Henry I at the Battle of Mortemer in 1054. This did not end the contention between them, though, as Henry I again attacked in 1057. The Battle at Varaville during that year nearly saw the death of the king, who had to flee from the capital. Henry I found himself and about half of his army on one side of the river, having barely escaped William and his men. All the king and his forces, those who had managed to escape, could do was watch as the floodwaters of the river rose, and the men who could not escape across the river were slaughtered by William's army.

When Henry I died in 1060, his son, Philip I, took over the throne. Just like William had been, Philip I was too young to actually rule the nation. The new king's guardian was Baldwin V of Flanders, who, by this time, was William's father-in-law. Philip I was only seven years old when he became king, and it was his mother, Anne of Kiev, who served as regent until he turned fourteen years old.

With such a young king on the throne, whose advisor and mother were not interested in continuing to fight, there was no longer any reason for the king and William to fight. These familial bonds were something that he had learned to wield to great effect, and this was just one more example of how William managed to resolve an issue without fighting. He is remembered for his military prowess, but his ability to forge alliances through marriage was just as strategic.

No longer having to worry about retaining his power in Normandy, William took this opportunity to finally take stock of his situation. Without a king who feared his power, William decided that he could continue his expansion, but it would mean focusing on somewhere new. As a distant relation to the king of England, it was clear to him where he should turn his attention next.

The problem was that, technically, he was a vassal to the French king. As a vassal, he could not attack another country without first trying to find a peaceful resolution. That meant that he would have to start with diplomacy, something that he had mastered nearly as well as military strategy. However, William knew that the likelihood of success was slim.

There was a second issue that would prove to be problematic, at least initially. France and England had some ties, but they largely had not attacked each other over the years. There was no obvious benefit of taking the English throne to the members of his nobility. He had to convince them that it would be worth the preparation and struggles to take the kingdom that had proven to be their equals in battle. This ended up being less complicated than William may have initially believed, as the promise of new lands and titles that would go to those who supported the venture persuaded a large number of the French nobility to join him.

His Claim to the Throne

By 1066, the fighting that had plagued Normandy because of the contention between William and the French King Henry I was over, and the new ruler of France allied with him to face the king of England. William's ostracization because of the status of his birth also drove him to seek additional approval, so he went to the pope. After receiving papal approval, he had everything in place to lay his claim to the English throne.

It was certainly true that William was related to Edward the Confessor. They were both related to Count Richard I of Normandy; Count Richard I of Normandy was Edward's grandfather and William's great-grandfather. They were distant relations, but William was a closer relation than Harold, whose sister had been married to Edward the Confessor. This logic was what had won William the support of so many.

Despite this, William had spread word that Edward had promised him the throne and that Harold Godwinson had pledged his allegiance to William during a visit to Normandy in 1064 CE. It was possible that this happened, as Harold had been in Normandy some years earlier. However, it is by no means certain that this actually happened. And if it did, it is possible that William had forced the oath out of him, meaning it was done against Harold's will.

William claimed that Edward had promised that he would be the heir back in 1051 when he went to visit England. While this is possible, Edward the Confessor did use this kind of promise to keep people in check, so whether or not he had meant it (if he had even made the promise in the first place) is not without a lot of doubt. During 1051, the Godwin family had been exiled from England, so it is possible that in his anger, Edward had promised the throne to William, though even that could have been to keep William from attacking while Edward was at his most vulnerable.

According to the Anglo-Saxons, Edward promising the throne to William was a lie to justify his actions. But despite England's protests, other kings sided with William. It was likely that they would have supported him regardless, as the idea of a throne going to someone who was not a blood relation to a ruler could have established a dangerous precedent. When Harold II of England refused to give up the throne, despite the decree of the pope, William had all of the justification that he needed to invade England. As King Harald Hardrada marched on the island without any backing by the rest of the continent, William began his preparations to attack the newly crowned king, Harold II, himself. Beginning in the summer of 1066, William found himself planning how to cross the English Channel and what the best strategy would be to expand his power into England. He did not have to worry too much about Normandy and the lands that he had taken because his connections within France and his reputation would keep his lands safe.

It is interesting to note that the pope had done more than just back William; he had also excommunicated Harold II. It is possible that Harold II did not take this well, and some say that he may have been disheartened by this apparent betrayal. Still, Harold did not relent in his claim, foreshadowing the events that would happen several centuries later under Henry VIII, who managed to finally break free from the Catholic Church.

Chapter 5 – Harold II of England

Perhaps the strongest claim to the English throne actually lay with the man who was coronated the day after Edward died, Harold Godwinson. His father had been integral in running the country and had worked with Edward the Confessor since he first became king. After his death, Harold took his father's place managing the secular aspects of the kingdom. His family may not have been related to the throne by blood, but they were a noble Anglo-Saxon family.

Early Life

Born in the early 1020s (usually estimated around 1022), Harold was the son of the Earl of Wessex, Godwin. The family was of noble Anglo-Saxon heritage that had been a part of the development of the nation for centuries, a tradition that had been strengthened under Edward the Confessor. Harold's mother, Gytha Thorkelsdóttir, had links to the Danish throne; her brother, Ulf Thorgilsson, had married Cnut's sister, Estrid. Harold had seven siblings, including Edith, the sister who married

King Edward. His brothers were given their own regions to manage, though things did not always go smoothly between Harold and his brothers.

When he was still in his early 20s, Harold was given the title of earl of East Anglia, giving him a large estate to control. During the beginning of the 1050s, Harold and his family became entangled in disagreements with King Edward, and the family members had to flee the country for a while, including Queen Edith. After leaving their lands, members of the Godwin family spent time in Ireland. Edward quickly learned just how little power he actually had without the powerful Godwins helping him. When he had been living in Normandy during his exile and the kingdom was under control by Cnut, the Godwin family had remained in England. Without the Godwins, Edward's grasp over his kingdom was tentative, and in addition, he now had to take care of the aspects of ruling that he had no interest in managing. The family had left in 1051, but they returned to their lands in 1052.

Following Godwin's death in 1053, Harold inherited the title of the earl of Wessex. Because of the new title, Harold was not allowed to keep his former title of earl of East Anglia because of the power imbalance it would have created between the earls of the kingdom. Edward the Confessor was the one who ordered Harold to give up his first earldom, but despite this, Harold was still the most powerful earl in England, and it could be argued the most powerful person in the kingdom, as Edward had allowed his father to largely run the country and continued to allow Harold to do so as well.

Internal Strife

During his time in assisting Edward the Confessor, Harold had been required to manage uprisings and problems within the kingdom. In 1063, he successfully attacked the king of Wales, Gruffydd ap Llywelyn, expanding Edward's kingdom into this smaller country. During this conquest in 1063, Harold's brother, Tostig, fought by his side. One attacked the people of Wales by sea, while the other approached them by land. As a result, Gruffydd went into exile. Fear of what Harold might do caused the people to turn on the king of Wales, and after capturing Gruffydd, they beheaded him and presented the head to Harold to show that they supported him. This cemented his position as the under-king to Edward, who did not participate in the endeavor.

Tostig had supported his brother in the fight against Wales, but he proved to be a poor leader. Between his ruthless nature and the over-taxation of the people in his region, Northumbria, the people became dissatisfied with him. A revolt began in 1065, and Tostig could not put it down. Harold was forced to step in and restore order in the northern realm. To do this, though, he had to strip his brother of his title and send Tostig into exile, something that Tostig did not take well. There were rumors that Harold had managed to instigate the revolt in a bid to further gain Edward's trust and a place on the throne following the king's death. However, there was never any substantial evidence of this rumor.

In 1065, Harold married the widow of the King Gruffydd ap Llywelyn, Ealdgyth. Not only did this help provide a connection to Wales, but she was also related to earls in the northern part of the kingdom. This helped to extend Harold's power, which would have been the only real reason for the marriage. Harold had been romantically attached to Edith the Fair, also known as Edith Swanneck, and together, they had five children. It is said that Harold had married Edith Swanneck, but the marriage between Harold and Ealdgyth was the one that was deemed to be legitimate in the eyes of the clergy, and so, Edith Swanneck was seen as a mistress.

Claim to the Throne

Like King Harald of Norway, Harold Godwinson did not have any blood claim to the throne. However, his sister had been the wife of Edward the Confessor, which gave him about as much claim to the throne as William the Bastard. Since Harold had been working with the rightful king for so long, he actually made the most sense as the next king. He was also of Anglo-Saxon ancestry, while William was not.

The people of England had been ruled by the Romans hundreds of years before, and they had been under constant attack by the Vikings for the last couple hundred years. They wanted to keep the royal family Anglo-Saxon instead of having another ruler who did not understand their customs or traditions. With Harold having already established himself as a capable leader, they firmly supported him.

Events in Normandy

According to William the Bastard, Harold had pledged to support his claim to the throne during a visit to Normandy in 1064 CE. Edward the Confessor was said to have sent Harold to Normandy to talk with William, though what they were supposed to discuss has been subject to debate. Some speculate that it was for William to express Edward's desire that William become his heir, which is mainly based on what William later claimed was the case. Some say that Normandy was not even Harold's destination and that he and his men were blown off course on a trip to France and were subsequently captured by William and his men.

During his time in Normandy, Harold actually helped William by fighting for William against the Conan II, Duke of Brittany. For his help, William knighted Harold, at least according to the recordings that were added to the Bayeux Tapestry. However, it is also said that the only reason that William allowed Harold to leave was that he forced Harold

Godwinson to promise that he would support William as the heir to the throne. This has been the account that has been passed down because William was the victor in the end, but that does not mean that the events actually occurred in the way that he claimed. For instance, the *Anglo-Saxon Chronicles* provide a completely different set of events of what happened in Normandy. According to their records, Harold's sole purpose in Normandy was to negotiate the release of English compatriots.

Either way, it is fairly clear that any oath that Harold took while in Normandy was done against his will and under duress. Both versions have reported that he was a captive of William's, though to different degrees. The fact that the oath was forced from him would have meant that it was not valid, and that is what the Anglo-Saxons believed.

History will never resolve exactly what happened during Harold's time in Normandy, though it is not entirely relevant. While they both had a better claim than King Harald of Norway, the best claim actually went to a living relative of King Æthelred II.

The Real Heir to the Throne

Edward may have died without any children, but his father had children from a previous marriage. They had been largely ignored because of how power-hungry Edward's mother, Emma of Normandy (King Æthelred II second wife), had been. She had been set on having her lineage on the throne, and she had ensured that by marrying Cnut after her first husband, King Æthelred II, died.

However, Edmund Ironside was King Æthelred II's eldest son, and it was his grandson, Edgar Ætheling, who had the best claim to the throne. Edmund's incredibly short reign saw England once again being ruled by a Viking usurper, pushing his rightful heir—his son named Edward the Exile, Edgar's father—out of the line of succession. King Æthelred II's second wife, Emma, would make sure that Edward the Exile would not rise to power, constantly putting her sons on the throne. However, as the second wife, her line should not have been the next on the throne. At the time of Edward the Confessor's death in 1066, Edgar was only a teenager. Many have speculated that Harold and other Anglo-Saxon nobles ensured that Edgar was kept from consideration, at least in part because of his age. Records of what happened were not kept, so it is only speculation as to what happened.

One strange thing to note was how quickly Harold's coronation had occurred following King Edward's death. It was not customary for a king to be crowned within a day of the death of the previous monarch. Given how rushed the coronation was, it appears that Harold was trying to ensure that there was no time for any arguments or issues to arise because Edward had been childless when he died. With as dubious as the claims had been, they were only getting murkier. It was the perfect opportunity for Harold to finally establish his family as the rulers of the country. Unfortunately, for him, the hasty coronation did not stop others from seeking to claim the throne for themselves.

Following Harold's death at the Battle of Hastings, it does appear that the Anglo-Saxons finally suggested Edgar Ætheling be the next king. At only fifteen years old, he really would not have stood a chance against the much older and experienced William. Instead of trying to take his rightful place on the throne, he would eventually serve both William I and his son, William II. As William worked to stamp out the numerous rebellions, Edgar Ætheling spent time in Scotland from 1068 to 1072 with King Malcolm III Canmore. The Scottish king would face off against the fierce Norman army and would end up submitting. Edgar Ætheling again submitted to William's reign. By 1086, Edgar Ætheling was trusted enough by William I to lead the Norman forces, who were sent to the southern Italian city of Apulia in order to conquer it.

Edgar Ætheling would go on one of the early Crusades before England went through another civil war. During the next civil war, Edgar sided with the Duke of Normandy against the current English king, Henry I. They lost, and little is known of what happened to the man who should have been the king of England after 1106.

Chapter 6 – Verification of Events and Preparations for War

One thing that historians today agree on regarding the events prior to Edward's death was that something he said during William's visit to England in 1051 had been misunderstood by William as a promise that he would be the next king. This had made him think that he would eventually gain the crown of England without having to lift a finger.

Initially, even the Normans were not happy with the idea of invading England, and William was criticized for drawing them into yet another fight. It was only with the promise of new lands and titles that the Normans were convinced to back William the Bastard as the next King of England. This did not mean that the preparations went as smoothly as William could have wanted. Once he realized what was coming, Harold Godwinson had no less difficulty in trying to convince his people of the imminent danger that was coming from Normandy.

William's Reaction to Edward's Death

Word of King Edward's death reached William very quickly, interrupting a hunt that he and his men had been preparing to take on his lands. Since the coronation of Harold had happened so quickly, William learned both of Edward's death and Harold's coronation at the same time.

His reaction is easy to guess, and it was poetically described around one hundred years after the events of 1066. Anger gripped William as he honestly believed that Edward had actually promised it to him. It is almost certain that Edward had not meant anything when he made the promise, as he had dangled the crown in front of others before and after William, but William also likely believed that he was the best choice, so he was convinced that it had been a guarantee that he would be the heir to the English throne. There is also a very good chance that this is why he had never sought to expand into England before—he thought that all he had to do was survive Edward; after that, he was guaranteed the English crown.

Enraged that Harold would allow himself to be coronated, William realized that the position he thought would automatically become his was not so easily claimed. However, war was not his initial reaction. The two men had fought together on the same side, and William was not willing to attack without attempting to find a peaceful, less costly method first. This could be because of how different the two regions were and how they faced questions of power and expansion. Much of William's life had revolved around fighting and war. Many believe that he was illiterate and that he and his people were far less educated than the Anglo-Saxons were (in their eyes, they were potentially even more barbaric than Harald Hardrada and his Vikings). While revolts and problems had occurred during Edward's time, they were often resolved quickly, keeping the country from devolving into civil war. By comparison, the earldoms of France were constantly fighting and had little identity as a whole. They constantly sought to protect their lands and expand into that of their neighbors. This was in stark contrast to the English under Edward and Harold, who had developed an identity of the nations and were proud to be a part of it. The earls of Edward's kingdom rarely fought each other, with unrest usually occurring when one of the earls wronged the people on their lands. William and the other earls saw the peasants living on their land more as objects and cared little about what happened to them. Though he was religious, William often put himself over even the Church, making him less than ideal as the leader of the more peaceful island kingdom.

The other problem had to do with William's pride. For years, he had been telling people in Normandy and elsewhere in the French kingdom that he was the heir to the English throne. Now that the king was dead, Harold's coronation made a mockery of what William had been saying. The fact that he felt wronged both by Edward and Harold ensured that he would act, though, to his credit, William did attempt to find a peaceful resolution first.

Whatever his initial reaction was, William did not react with immediate wrath. Instead of storming off to attack the kingdom, he sent word to Harold, hoping to hear that it had been a mistake. Harold was adamant that he had been chosen by Edward and that he had already been made the king. There was just no going back now that the coronation had occurred. Of course, there are many questions about just how rapidly Harold had ensured that coronation. Even if he had been chosen to be king by Edward the Confessor and the people who had the final say (the Witan, also known as the Witenagemot, the Anglo-Saxon council which determined succession, resolved land grants, issued charters, managed church matters, and held considerable sway over the direction of the kingdom), the coronation was suspiciously fast, and no coronation had ever happened so quickly, especially with so many questions about who the rightful king was. Typically, those who felt they had a claim to the throne were given time to put forth their claim, but Harold had ensured that no one else was given that time. However, the death of King Edward around the religious holiday of Epiphany meant that all of the important people were already present. It is possible that the coronation was rushed because everyone was already there, and putting it off would have made them either have to remain or return soon after the holiday. In the end, it could have been an issue of convenience over any rush on Harold's part. Since what has come down was from the Norman perspective, the real reason for the rapidity of Harold's coronation could have been obscured by the conquerors to give William's claim more legitimacy and to erode Harold's claim.

Some historians say that William had made a second effort to peacefully resolve the dispute by asking if Harold would marry his daughter. This is dubious, for if William had tried to ensure that Harold would fulfill a promise to marry his daughter, it would be out of character for the Norman earl. Once he felt insulted, especially how publicly he had been humiliated when word arrived of Edward's death, William often prepared for war. He had already given Harold a chance for peace; offering a second option does not seem likely. However, if this did occur, broken betrothals were entirely common at the time. Considering the age difference between Harold (44 years old) and William's daughter Agatha (about 8 years old), it would have meant that Harold would have had to wait until she reached puberty to marry her. He also already had Edith Swanneck (who the church considered to be a mistress), whose relationship is perhaps comparable to a common-law wife today. And not long after his coronation, he married Ealdgyth of Mercia. So, marriage to William's daughter was not really an option.

Harold did have the opportunity, though, to apologize more sincerely or to try to come up with a compromise. He had built much of his reputation on his ability to come to peaceful terms with his adversaries when it was possible. For a man with this kind of reputation, this was perhaps his greatest failing when it came to the issue of succession. However, Harold also had to abide by what the Witan said, and they did not have a reason to apologize for his coronation. As far as they were concerned, William did not have a claim to the throne, and they felt no need to try to pacify him. With this final denial of any claim William or his family may have had, William decided there was only one way to resolve the damage that had been done to his pride.

Within a month of his coronation, King Harold realized how much of a mistake it had been to be as unmoving as he had been when dealing with William. Whatever their relationship was before January of 1066, they were now enemies. And William was a very dangerous enemy to have.

A Hard Sell and War Preparations

Both rulers had their own problems with trying to convince people about the necessity of the war. For William, the problem was in selling the idea of going to war, especially after he had already told everyone that he was the English heir. Fighting to take lands so far from home had never been something that the Normans had considered, and there was no obvious reason for them to invade England. There was more than enough political intrigue and fighting at home to keep them occupied without risking to go so far away to unfamiliar lands. Initially, it seemed more like a vanity war that William was dragging them into.

Meanwhile, King Harold spent months trying to make his people understand the grave danger they were in as he had already seen what William could do. The southern parts of the kingdom were not accustomed to preparing for danger, as they often waited until the last minute when the danger was visible to them. Much of the kingdom operated that way because, apart from the Viking raids, they had lived more peacefully than the people of the continental kingdoms.

To rally people to his cause, William held up the relationship he had with Edward, which had been positive. Because of the promise William felt Edward had made to him, he worked to convince the people that the throne had been stolen from him. The reluctance of the nobles was relatively quickly broken down as William promised them that the English lands would be divided among them, proving that William had little intention of upholding the power structure in England. Given the fact that the English nobles and the Witan had given Harold the crown, there was likely some resentment. Once William procured the consent of the pope to attack, he was able to put his plan of attack in action.

By the summer of 1066, the English were more than willing to listen to Edward's warnings, and he had amassed a much larger force to face the danger he knew was coming from Normandy. According to the *Anglo-Saxon Chronicle*, it was the largest force that had ever been gathered in the kingdom. The army was made up of nobles and their housecarls (similar to a knight). According to the Vikings, who had encountered the fierce housecarls, they were as capable as two soldiers. Unfortunately, there were not many housecarls, and the kingdom did not have a standing army, as armies were too expensive (and largely unnecessary in England). Much of the army was composed of citizens who were required by law to serve in the military for two months a year. There were also some peasants who could be ordered to serve in the military by the earl or the person in charge of a particular region.

Harold also managed to build an unprecedented naval force that included ships that followed the designs commonly used by the Vikings to carry cargo. They were not as effective as the Viking longships that were used in raids, but when the ships were originally commissioned, which was before Harold had become king, warfare had not been the primary concern.

The problem was that the first battle did not come from William. It was King Harald and Harold's brother Tostig who would prove to be the first to strike in a bid to take the throne.

Chapter 7 – The Invasion of the Norwegian King Harald Hardrada

Though he had the least claim to the English throne, King Harald Hardrada was undeterred. There had never been a point in his life where he would simply give up without trying. Though he had not been as successful at uniting the continental kingdom that Cnut had managed, Harald felt that he could take on the English with more success. The idea that he could succeed was bolstered by the fact that he was able to get someone on his side who knew King Harold II well—his brother Tostig.

Eyeing the Isle and Forming Alliances

Just as Norway's political climate had drastically changed during Harald's time away, England had changed significantly after King Cnut's death. His sons, Harold Harefoot and then Harthacnut, had not ruled for too long, a combined seven years between them. After their reigns, England was back under the control of the Anglo-Saxons, first going to Edward the Confessor and then Harold Godwinson. No longer under the control of any Viking king, the Anglo-Saxons had become accustomed to being under the control of one of their own, and they were far less likely to welcome any foreign invaders.

Like he had done when trying to take Denmark from Magnus I, Harald looked for people close to King Harold with whom he could ally. And in doing so, he found Tostig Godwinson. Unlike his brother Harold, Tostig was not on good terms with King Edward the Confessor, resulting in his removal from his Northumbrian earldom. Tostig felt that his brother had betrayed him as it was Harold who ultimately had him pushed out as the earl of Northumbria. He had been a harsh leader during his time as earl, and Harold really did not have much choice but to remove him to end the Northumbrian civil war that had resulted from discontentment under Tostig's rule. King Edward may have been willing to allow Tostig to continue, but Harold had greater control over the secular rule of the lands, much as his father had before him. It is not certain why Harold was so willing to turn on his brother, but it is likely that the pressure and power of the rebels helped to persuade him that his brother could not manage the region peacefully. While Tostig had helped to bring some stability to the region, his methods had caused the revolt. Feeling betrayed, Tostig went to Flanders and then sought to provide assistance to attack England when the opportunity arose. In a strange twist of fate, he had initially offered his services to William of Normandy. However, William did not feel that he needed Tostig's help as Tostig's plans often were not well thought out, and he also seemed a bit unstable.

Knowing that he would need more help than Tostig could provide, Harald also allied with the chieftains in Shetland and Orkney. They were Scottish, but the lands were under the control of Norway. Feeling that he had enough men to be victorious, Harald finally made his move and began the invasion of England.

The Battle of Fulford (September 20ᵗʰ, 1066)

With 10,000 men, Harald landed in northern England at the mouth of the River Tees. Initially, he attacked using the traditional lightning strikes of his people, tormenting the English people who lived along the coast. Harald and his forces worked their way south to Scarborough, where they burned the town down because the townspeople put up fierce resistance to the invaders. Following this brutal display, the people of the Northumbrian region were far less willing to fight back against the invaders.

The destruction that King Harald of Norway was bringing along the coast soon became impossible for King Harold II of England to ignore, so he deployed forces north to face the invaders. Sending 5,000 men, the Anglo-Saxon king faced off against the battle-hardened Vikings at Fulford. Harald's men had the advantage, both because his forces were twice the size of the English king's and because the terrain was marshy, which was easier for Harald's people to navigate.

For the first time since they had invaded England, Harald and his men achieved a decisive victory against the Anglo-Saxons.

The Tide Turns at the Battle of Stamford Bridge (September 25ᵗʰ, 1066)

King Harold II had only been king of England for almost ten months by this point. Desperate to keep the country under his control, he marched to the front of his forces and pushed them to move more than 190 miles north to where the Viking invaders had stationed themselves.

King Harold and King Harald met again at the Battle of Stamford Bridge.

Much of this story was told by Snorri Sturluson, the author of *King Harald's Saga*, so some of the events should be taken with a grain of salt. What is certain is that Harald had not expected the English to march north to engage his troops, giving Harold II the element of surprise. It is likely that what the Viking king was expecting was an exchange of hostages, as was typically agreed to after a major battle. Instead, he found an English army now marching toward him and his army, and the English army was much larger than it had been at Fulford. It is estimated that King Harold II had amassed a force of around 13,000 men. In comparison, the Vikings had between 7,000 to 9,000 men, although some of these men joined later in the battle. This was because the Vikings were resting, meaning they were not equipped to fight, with most of them not even wearing their heavy armor, and the Viking forces were spread across two sides of the local river, the River Derwent.

The Viking forces that were on the wrong side of the river tried to cross the bridge to their armory so that they could fight together as a unit, but the English charged them, killing many before the Vikings could return to the main part of the camp.

An interesting legend from this time (recorded in the *Anglo-Saxon Chronicle*) relayed a story of a single Viking standing on the bridge to create a choke point against the English. He was able to kill forty Anglo-Saxons before one of them snuck under the bridge and killed him with a spear.

By the time the English forces crossed the bridge, the Vikings had had enough time to regroup and form a shield wall against them. The chaos that ensued must have irked Harald. Going into a berserker rage, he threw himself into the advancing English army. It is said that during his rage, the king was struck in the neck by an arrow, and he perished on the field. Without their king, the Vikings no longer had the drive to continue to face the Anglo-Saxon forces. Harold's brother Tostig was also killed during this battle, giving the Vikings no claim to the throne.

King Harald is sometimes referred to as the last of the great Vikings. He did not back down and continued many of the tactics for which his people had become famous. Sometimes he divided his people, while at other times he sought to unite them, always under his own banner. Unwavering in his courage and sometimes obstinate to a fault, he was the last Viking king who embodied the virtues and ideals of the Vikings as we know them today.

Chapter 8 – William Arrives in England

The last time England was successfully invaded was 1066, a year that had already seen so much turmoil and uncertainty. The events leading up to William's arrival in England actually played into his favor. King Harold II and his men had recently fought with King Harald in the north. Whether or not he knew about King Harald's attack, William's timing could not have been better, for it was on September 28th, 1066, that he landed in southern England at Pevensey Bay.

Significant Events and Battles of 1066

Amitchell125 at English Wikipedia, CC BY 3.0 <https://creativecommons.org/licenses/by/3.0>, via Wikimedia Commons https://commons.wikimedia.org/wiki/File:Norman-conquest-1066.svg

William's First Actions

The omens were good for William and his planned conquest. After having waited for nearly two months to make the crossing based on the right winds, those winds and favorable conditions finally began one day after the Battle of Stamford Bridge. This meant that Harold II was far to the north, although it is unlikely that William knew that as he and his men left the continent the next day. One day later, they made landfall on the island. The Battle of Samford Bridge was on September 25th, 1066; the Norman invasion began on September 28th, 1066. The timing could not have been more perfect for William, and little could have made the timing worse for Harold II. With this situation, the Normans could have easily believed that this was a sign that William was the rightful king, adding further religious righteousness to their cause.

Upon his arrival in England, William began to raid the towns and villages in the area. This was effective, not only because it brought terror to the Anglo-Saxons, but it was also the area that Harold's family came from. William had been aboard the ship *Mora* when they landed, the largest and fastest of the 700 or more ships used during the invasion, and it is likely that he did not know too much about the coastline, as they had only planned the invasion for a few months. Until January 1066, he had never had any reason to survey the lands or to consider an invasion. However, he likely would have known of its importance to Harold II. Some historians speculate that the reason they landed in Pevensey was because of the tides. They would not want to sail out of the area against the tides, so they docked and began their invasion, attacking those in the surrounding area.

At the time, Pevensey was primarily a market town, not a village. With the summer over, there were fewer soldiers around to protect the people in the area as they had gone home after the end of summer. When William and the Normans invaded, the people in England could see them coming, but they did not have any protection against them. Since most of them were merchants, farmers, and ranchers, their only real course of action was to try to hide from the invaders.

In the Bayeux Tapestry, the men are shown without their helmets at this time. This would indicate that they did not expect much resistance in the beginning. William would likely have known about the different towns, villages, and populations in the area and what they were likely to encounter. The tapestry would later depict the Normans as having helmets when they fought at the Battle of Hastings, so it was very likely that the Normans knew they were primarily going to be conducting raids instead of actually fighting when they arrived. This would have given them the base they needed for their men. Considering they arrived in a market town, they were able to better supply the troops with food and potable water, as they had not been well provisioned prior to leaving the continent.

Knowing that they had at least a few days before Harold II and his army could arrive (not knowing that they would actually have a couple of weeks), they were able to build a small round fort just inside one of the Roman walls built several centuries earlier. The fort was constructed of wood, and they dug a trench around it within a matter of a couple of days. This provided them with a place where they could plan their next moves.

Initially, William set out with William FitzOsbern, who was a distant cousin, and several of his knights to scout the area after the construction of the fort. They departed on horseback, but their lack of familiarity with the land soon proved to be a source of embarrassment. The men returned from their reconnaissance mission by foot because of how difficult it was for the horses on the terrain. The lands of Normandy were nothing like the lands of southern England, a factor that the Normans had not considered. The lands were wetter, with a lot of marshland in the area, making it much harder to traverse.

Though they had already created a fort, the Normans decided to leave the area. The embarrassing scouting incident, which was certainly undignified for the short-tempered Norman leader, was not the only reason to leave Pevensey, though. Only one reliable road went in and out of the area, and it had been built while the Romans had been in control of the area. This road did eventually lead to London, but there was no other direction for them to go if needed.

When they left, the Normans were quick to start striking fear in the hearts of the people. Some of the villages in the area were left alone, but many were not so lucky. One of the ways that historians have determined where the Normans raided was through the value placed on villages and towns in the area according to the Domesday Book, which was commissioned over a decade later (more information about this book is located in chapter 11). The book reflects the value of the population areas and the region, and some of the villages were marked as *wasta*, indicating that they had been laid to waste during the invasion. The trail of Norman destruction would go from Pevensey all the way to Hastings, which was where they would finally face their enemy and change the entire trajectory of the future of England.

Some historians have postulated that William encouraged his men to conduct raids as a way of drawing Harold down to the area. However, it is more likely that they conducted warfare in England the same they had anywhere else. Fighting on the continent had included raiding and pillaging every place that they went, so it would have taken a major intervention to stop the men from doing what they likely saw as natural. The fighters on the continent saw the slaughtering and destruction of civilians and towns as a part of warfare, not as a crime as it is viewed today. This is why it is somewhat ironic that William had promised lands to the Normans since population centers were destroyed upon their arrival. Then again, it is likely that the people who had been promised lands would have known that rebuilding would be necessary, making it a calculated risk that they were willing to make.

The Normans again constructed a fort that they could use in Hastings. From it, the Normans raided all of the surrounding areas. Only two towns were not destroyed during this time: Hastings and Westfield. Hastings was spared because they had made it their hub. However, historians are not sure why Westfield was spared the same treatment as the other villages in the area.

Harold's Mistake – Disbanding the Army at the End of Summer

Nearly as soon as they had finished eliminating the threat of King Harald and Tostig, Harold II and his men received word that the Normans had invaded in the south. Having spent time with William of Normandy a few years previously, and then engaging in their tense exchange following Harold II's coronation, the king likely knew that the Norman invasion was a serious threat to his crown, as well as his people. Harold would have known that he could not waste time.

The timing of the invasion was terrible for King Harold II for two reasons, firstly because of how it dovetailed with a northern invasion. The other was that Harold had been waiting in the southern part of the country for most of the summer because he knew that William's arrival was imminent. The question was when he would invade, not if he would. Harold had men stationed both on land and at sea for most of the summer in preparation for the inevitable. At the time, standing armies really did not exist. The men who were stationed in the south had to return home for the harvest, so on September 8th, Harold disbanded the militia.

It was only a few weeks later that Harald Hardrada invaded, causing Harold to rush north with what men he had. Despite their decisive victory, the Anglo-Saxons had suffered great losses of the men who were available to fight. The king's only real option was to rally men to the Anglo-Saxon cause as they marched south as quickly as possible.

Many of the earls in the northern parts of the country chose not to assist with the southern invasion as they did not feel that they were directly threatened by the invaders. Still, the king did enlist people from the areas that they passed through on their way to confront the invaders. As soon as he and his current force reached London, the king sent word out to other earls that he needed additional support to stop the latest invasion. Perhaps as word of the chaos and destruction that the Normans had been wrecking on his former Wessex earldom reached him, Harold II became anxious to move out and stop him. The knights and men of the higher social class rode south on horses, while anyone else who joined them traveled on foot. Harold II had lost a large number of his housecarls in the northern battle, meaning that he was in a much weaker position when he marched south than he had been when he first headed north to confront Harald Hardrada.

Some of his supporters would criticize the king for his hasty decision to attack soon after they arrived near Hastings. There were still men who were responding to the call when Harold II decided to engage the Normans. It is perhaps this decision that would lead to the events of that October day, but it is also possible that waiting for more support would not have changed the events. What is known is that King Harold II would not delay his attack when he was within striking distance of his latest enemy.

Chapter 9 – The Battle of Hastings and William's Coronation

At the beginning of September 1066, there was nothing particularly interesting about Hastings, nothing that would have even hinted at the pivotal event that would occur about a month and a half later. When William and the Normans set up in the area, they all but destroyed the area, so they would not have been able to remain there over the course of the winter.

Fortunately for the Normans, though, Harold II and his men arrived before the winter began. The battle actually occurred about six and a half miles away, in the small town known as Battle today. It was located northwest of Hastings, but as one of the few places that still remained in the region, the battle was named after the place where William and his men had stationed themselves.

Today, we are accustomed to wars dragging out for years, with our leaders sitting far from the fighting. During the Middle Ages, however, the leaders fought their own battles since soldiers would often not follow a man who was not willing to put his life on the line to show his dedication to his claims. This meant that if the leader of one of the armies died, the end of a battle could be a decisive victory for the other side. However, as William would find out, winning a battle and killing King Harold II was not the end of the war.

Still, the Battle of Hastings did successfully answer the question of who would reign as king. A year that had begun with the death of King Edward the Confessor would end with the coronation of King William I. Had Harold II been victorious at Hastings, the history of the island nation would have been very different from what we know today.

On the Eve of Battle

Harold II and his men had marched about 200 miles within a week to reach Hastings, which was an impressive feat back then. This was an average of thirty miles every day, which started about a week after Harold stopped in London. By October 13th, both of the armies were in southern England, about eight miles apart from each other, which shows just how quickly Harold II had marched his men down to stop William.

Given that the battle happened about 950 years ago, there is a lot that we do not know, such as how many men followed William and Harold II into battle. The numbers given for both varies because it is unlikely that either side actually took the time to count their forces before the battle started. According to modern estimates, it is thought that Harold II had between 7,000 to 12,000 men, while William had between 5,000 and 13,000 men.

Based on the scenes depicted on the Bayeux Tapestry, both men had established similar forces, including cavalry and archers. However, Harold II had fewer archers than his enemy, which gave William a distinct advantage, besides his men being more well-rested. Some speculate that

Harold II would have had a greater contingent of archers if he had taken a more measured approach. Archers would almost certainly have moved on foot, which meant that many of them were likely still making their way south. It is almost certain that Harold II had pressed south as quickly as possible to protect the earldom that had been in his family for so long. Had he been less hasty, his men may have been better matched against the effective Norman archers who used crossbows.

Final Preparations

When the morning of October 14th began, the two leaders were setting up their men in formations that they felt would play best against the strategies and forces of the other. Harold II and his higher-ranking men had traveled on horse, but the English did not typically use horses in battle. William and the Normans did. This meant that the Normans would be sending their cavalry in to fight against a thick wall of Anglo-Saxon soldiers on foot.

The Anglo-Saxon forces were established in a long line that is estimated to have been about half a mile long. They were stationed on a hill, giving them the upper ground. Their men had shields, meaning that their defense was more like a shield wall, which would have been incredibly difficult for the Norman cavalry to penetrate. To thwart the cavalry, the Anglo-Saxons had chosen to sacrifice maneuverability because the men were lined up almost shoulder to shoulder.

William had several different peoples to manage, which included the Normans, Bretons, and French forces. He stationed them based on their origins, with the Normans acting as the core of his forces. The other two groups were placed on the west and east. In addition to dividing his forces based on where they had learned to fight, the soldiers were put in formation based on their role in the fight. Archers were placed in the front to take down as many of the Anglo-Saxon men in the shield wall as possible. The next part of their forces was the infantry, followed by the knights who were to ride in on their horses. Once the archers had weakened the wall, the infantry would scatter them, and then the cavalry would kill the men who remained.

This showed two very different approaches to fighting. William and his men valued mobility and the flexibility to move across the lands. In contrast, Harold II and his men were more like the woods behind them. Their success required them to hold strong and to resist breaking against the highly mobile Normans. This is likely what caused the battle to continue longer than other battles of the era. Neither side had fought a battle against an enemy with such a different approach to their own. The Anglo-Saxon approach was more like the Roman fighting style, where soldiers stood in tight formation, while the Normans used a style that was more like what we associate with the Middle Ages.

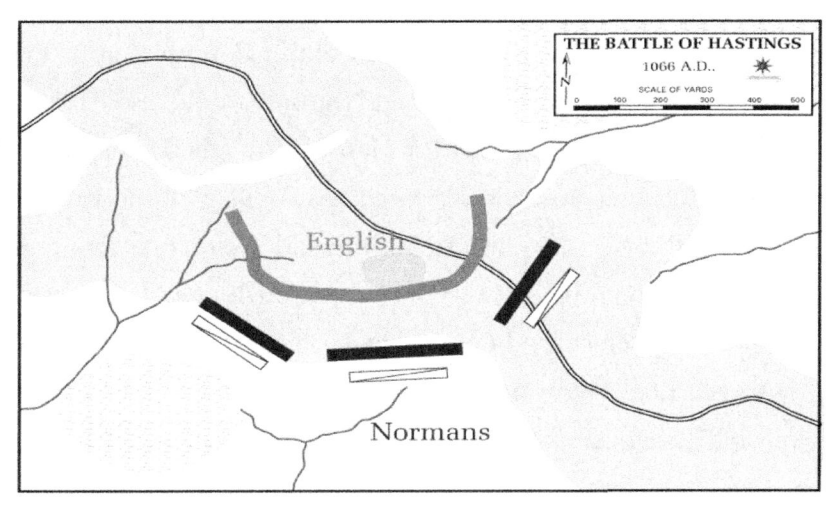

English and Norman Formations
https://commons.wikimedia.org/wiki/File:Battle_of_Hastings,_1066.png

The Fighting Starts – One of the Longest Battles at That Time

During the 11th century, battles usually only lasted a couple of hours. With all of the heavy gear and with so many men, fighting for long periods of time was generally detrimental. The Battle of Hastings would not follow the typical battle duration, though, as it lasted for nearly the entire day.

According to the Norman version of events, William surprised Harold and his men. This is probably an exaggerated or entirely inaccurate account, as Harold and his men were in position for the battle. It would not be out of place for propaganda to occur in order to try to give the victorious William greater glory and more credit than was actually earned.

According to another account, both sides sounded the trumpets, initiating the battle at 9 a.m. The grounds before them would have been fairly easy to maneuver, something that was not true of some of the surrounding areas. As William had found out in Pevensey, not all of the terrain was suited for cavalry or fighting. Not only would this have been a reason to settle in Hastings to wait for Harold II to attack, but it also gave his man better grounds to fight. However, the strategy of the English was to give themselves an area where they could more quickly retreat if needed. Behind the English were woods, though their formation was meant to be the protection they needed in the battle. If they needed to flee, the woods might have provided them with a better means of escape since it would have been more difficult for the cavalry to chase them in the bramble.

When the trumpets sounded, the Norman archers began to shoot a volley of their arrows against the wall of Anglo-Saxon warriors. The Anglo-Saxons responded nearly immediately as the Norman archers stepped out of the way. While they did not have many archers, they were armed with javelins and other weapons they could throw. It appears that some of the other projectiles that they launched against the invaders were sticks that had stones attached to them and, more interestingly, axes. William's plan to scatter Harold's men after the initial volley was quickly proven to be less effective than he had expected. Harold's men not only repelled the Norman foot soldiers but their cavalry as well.

Considering the first noted action of the battle was done by the archers, it is expected that the first fatalities were likely on the Anglo-Saxon side. Given that the records today come from the conquering side, the first death that was recorded belonged to the Normans. According to some accounts, the first person to die (at least on the Norman side) was someone close to the king—his jester named Taillefer.

This unexpected result caused panic among William's men. As some of them turned to retreat from a wall of soldiers that had not broken as expected, those behind them thought that the battle was turning against them. Some even thought that perhaps William had been killed during the initial skirmish. Parts of the wall broke as some of the Anglo-Saxons chased the fleeing men. When William went charging into the fray, his forces realized that he had not been killed. Soon, the men who had broken from the shield wall were eliminated as the invaders took heart in William's charge against the enemy.

There is a lot of speculation about what the Anglo-Saxons could have done differently that would have changed the events of what happened next. If the shield wall had pushed forward instead of breaking to pursue the Normans, they might have been successful. It is also said that they could have moved back together, holding the line that had already proven to be nearly impenetrable to William and his men. However, the Anglo-Saxons allowed themselves to be partially divided after having withstood the initial onslaught.

Despite this mistake, the wall did reform, and it remained strong over the course of the day, a feat that was likely physically punishing as they were limited in their movements. The Norman reports of the events showed their awe at how well-trained the English were against their advances.

After hours of fighting, William decided to use what he had learned from the first hours of the battle against the Anglo-Saxons. Ordering his cavalry to leave the field, he drew out more of the men who had been standing strong against them. After a greater portion of the shield wall had been broken, William ordered his men to turn and annihilate those who had broken away.

This second wave occurred after a long day of fighting. After this second wave of attacks proved to be successful against them, the English saw no way out but to surrender.

The only thing that is certain is that Harold II died that day. What happened to him has been a source of debate, with some saying that he was killed by an arrow to the eye or the neck. Others say he was cut down on the battlefield. The loyal soldiers of his royal guard did continue to fight without him for a while, as they did not see the invader as being a legitimate king. They gathered around the body of Harold II and fought until the very end. There was a defensive action carried out by the Anglo-Saxons at a site known as the "Malfosse," but it is unknown what happened there, except for the fact that they seriously wounded Eustace II of Boulogne before being defeated.

After fighting for most of the day, and with their king dead, the shield wall had finally dissolved. The Anglo-Saxons broke and tried to flee. A large portion of those who fled reached a rampart that would provide them with some protection against the Normans who were pursuing them. With the light waning, the Normans found themselves in trouble as they could not really see, and the grounds were not familiar to them. Struggling through the long grass in the growing darkness, many of them ended up struggling and falling through the less sturdy, marshy grounds. It became too difficult for them to progress, which gave the surviving Anglo-Saxons one final advantage, as the English were able to make short work of many of the men who had tried to pursue them.

Unfortunately for the English, it was not enough. They had lost their king and many of the nobility who had followed him south.

The battle had lasted an unimaginable nine hours, with both sides exhausted by the time the fighting ceased. The Norman's mobility had allowed them to try some deceptive tactics to lure the Anglo-Saxons to break their ranks, which had some mild success. However, that would have taken a real toll on them as they would have had to repeatedly go up the hill where the English had formed their line. William himself was said to have lost three horses during the repeated charges. It is unknown when King Harold II had been killed, though some say that it was likely during the last Norman charge. With the English continuing to fight even after his death, the Normans could not have been sure of their victory until the very end of the battle. It was clear that the two sides were evenly matched, and any small changes in their forces or strategies could have completely changed the end results.

Harold II Laid to Rest

Just like King Harold II's death was obscured by different stories of his demise, the events surrounding the fate of his remains are not fully known. According to some stories, his mother had offered to pay a large sum of gold for his body so that he could be properly buried. However, William refused to return the body.

According to another story, Harold's long-time partner, Edith Swanneck, had gone to the site of the battle to identify him. He had been so badly mutilated that it was nearly impossible to identify him, so only his lover could say for certain that the corpse was his. If this story is true, then it would have been almost certain that he had not been killed by an arrow but by repeated attacks by the Normans on the battlefield.

In a third version, the one that was most widely repeated in the 12th century, said that he was finally laid to rest in Waltham Holy Cross located in Essex. This would later prove to be untrue as the tomb was opened to reveal that his remains were not there.

There is even a version of events that indicate just how difficult it was for him to accept defeat; according to this version, Harold had not been killed but had gone on to live elsewhere as a hermit until he was old. This is absolutely untrue, but it would have likely been something that William would have encouraged others to believe.

In all likelihood, the first story is the most likely scenario. By denying the Anglo-Saxons their king's body, William denied them a spiritual place around which they could rally. Stories were able to spring up around what had happened, some which even cast doubt on the fact that Harold II died during this battle. This denied the king his status as a martyr for the cause of the Anglo-Saxons. Whatever happened to Harold's body is lost to time due to the rumors and speculation about its fate.

Chapter 10 – Rebelling against the New King and the Consequences of Doing So

Harold II may have been killed during the Battle of Hastings, but the Anglo-Saxons were not willing to simply accept William of Normandy as their king. He had never lived in the country, did not have a legitimate claim in their eyes, and he had killed the king the Witan had elected. This led to a lot of resistance against William and his nobles.

A March across the South

Harold II and two of his brothers were killed during the Battle of Hastings, removing some of the best protectors of the Wessex earldom. Without their protectors, the more pastoral areas of southern England offered little challenge against the Normans. Places like Dover, Canterbury, and Winchester quickly fell to William and his forces. Then he turned his attention to the only place that could really hope to withstand his march across the region—London. Without their king to rally them, the people of London could not put up the kind of fight that was required to keep William from finally conquering the capital. By Christmas Day, William the Bastard was crowned William I. However, taking over the southern portions of the kingdom did not mean that the rest of the realms would accept him. And the other earls were not the only problem William would face. Edgar Ætheling was chosen by some to rule, but he was still just a teenager at the time. His ability to win would have been small, and he did not seem eager to press his claim to the throne.

It is interesting to consider how little he was actually prepared for what would happen after he became king of England. For a man who blindly believed a vague promise that he would be the next king, William I did precious little to understand the realm that he was going to rule. He did not have much of an understanding of the power structures in the country, nor did he understand his enemies. All of the problems that Edward the Confessor and Harold II had faced in ruling the lower kingdom on the island (Scotland was an entirely different nation at this time) would become unexpected issues for the new ruler.

Perhaps one of the best omens of how much difficulty he would encounter happened on the day that should have been celebratory: the day of William I's coronation.

A New King

Though William would continue to fight, the Battle of Hastings all but ensured he would be made king, no matter how the Anglo-Saxons felt about him. And on Christmas Day 1066, he was crowned king.

There are two primary records, the Bayeux Tapestry and the *Anglo-Saxon Chronicle*, that we can use to get a better glimpse at the chaos that occurred during 1066. However, neither of them provides details about the coronation. It is believed that the tapestry once included William I's coronation, but the end of the tapestry has been lost. The *Anglo-Saxon Chronicle* manuscripts are largely silent on this period. It is likely that they were upset by the loss of so many of their nobles and the success of an invader who had never shown an interest in their lands until Edward the Confessor had died.

William of Poitiers would write about the coronation and other events several years after William's victory. From this account, we have more details of the coronation, though there are definitely aspects that should be taken with several large grains of salt. According to him, "all shouted their joyful assent, with no hesitation, as if heaven had granted them one mind and one voice." In this, he also says that the English were celebrating their new king and were happy to be his subjects. Considering the little that was said about it in the *Anglo-Saxon Chronicle*, it is almost certain that this is little more than propaganda. While the Normans who were to get lands out of the conquest would have cheered for William, there was no reason for the English to welcome him. The new king was soon to give their lands away to foreigners who had backed him. He was just another invader usurping their throne under a claim that they did not believe. Perhaps the only reason why they would agree to William being king was in the hopes that they could minimize their losses under this new, more barbaric king.

William of Poitiers may have portrayed the cries as those of "joyful assent," but the series of events that followed it is a much more likely indicator of the proper interpretation of any cries from outside of the abbey where the new king was crowned. Guards in the abbey quickly exited to see what was happening, and once outside, they thought that the cries were a sign of treachery. In response, they began to set fire to the homes in the immediate area, lighting the city on fire. People began trying to fight the flames, losing interest in the coronation because of the fear of losing everything they owned.

This turned out to be an apt beginning to William I's reign. The lands around him burned, yet he continued with his plans forward. The first five years would prove to be the most difficult, largely because of his ignorance of the people and their problems. In response to the Anglo-Saxon's rejection of him, William and his men would plunder the country, claiming the wealth that the English had accumulated over the years. Even if they had accepted him, William had made promises to the Normans and others on the continent to get them to back his invasion. Plundering the wealth of the island was nearly a certainty because he had to make good on these promises. This would have given the native peoples a reason to keep rejecting him until he finally and brutally put down their attempts to overthrow them.

That Christmas Day in 1066 was an ominous sign of just what was to come.

Constant Troubles from the Natives, Long-standing Enemies, and an Unlikely Alliance

The Anglo-Saxons were not eager to welcome an invader, and this was quickly shown in repeated attacks against the Normans. The remaining members of the Godwin family, particularly Harold II's children, caused issues for William I. His sons instigated two of their own invasions after taking refuge in Ireland, where their father had spent his year of exile under Edward the Confessor. The earls of the northern realms were no less accepting, and a rebellion against William began in York. The new king was able to stop both of the Godwin invasions and the rebellion. The York rebellion proved to be more difficult, though, so William I ended up employing the barbaric tactics that were frequently used on the continent to put down the rebellion. Over the winter of 1069 and into the beginning of 1070, he took a scorched-earth approach to terrifying and crippling those who denied his claim. Like he had done in the south during the initial invasion, William burned villages to the ground, destroyed crops, and slaughtered the livestock.

Over time, nearly all of the old Anglo-Saxon families who had ruled over the different regions were removed in favor of Normans. To ensure that they were protected, William the Conqueror had castles constructed all around his kingdom. This was meant to provide places where his faithful followers would be safe, as soldiers could be stationed across the lands that were rejecting his rule.

William's victory near Hastings did not quell the problems of the countries that were frequent antagonists to the Anglo-Saxon people. While William I was fighting against Harold's children and against the York rebellion, he also faced attacks from Wales. Harold II had managed to subdue them, but they saw an opportunity to strike back against the new English king. William successfully repelled those attacks, but he did not take control of the country.

The people of Wales were not the only ones who saw the conquest as an opportunity. The Vikings had been a constant thorn in the side of Britain, and following William's coronation, they again started to raid the coast, as they had been doing on and off for centuries. Over the centuries, the Vikings had developed a strategy of raiding England whenever there were signs of problems in the country. Obviously, the changing of hands of the throne was not an opportunity that they could ignore. From their perspective, it was the perfect time to test out the new king who clearly did not know the history behind their attacks and so would likely not know how best to counter them.

The Vikings soon found an unlikely ally in the people who had once been staunchly opposed to them—the Anglo-Saxon nobles. An alliance was formed in September 1069 between King Sweyn II of Denmark and the English rebels who wanted the kingdom restored to their people. The Danish king sent 300 ships to York, led by his brother Asbjørn, where they were welcomed by the half-great-nephew of Edward the Confessor, Edgar Ætheling, who had begun a rebellion in York earlier that year but managed to escape unscathed. Together, the Vikings and the Anglo-Saxon rebels captured many of the commanders, who were then ransomed off to fund the fighting. Most of the troops who were not ransomed, whether because their family could not pay or because the troops were of common birth, were killed outright.

When William received word of this, he marched an army to York, only to find that the Vikings had already departed. The Danes had fled along the River Trent with a substantial amount of wealth that they had taken from the city and surrounding area. As he did not have a fleet, William could not pursue the Danes. The only recourse he had was the traditional Anglo-Saxon method of repulsing the Vikings—he had to pay them to leave (since generally all the Vikings sought was wealth from their raids). Asbjørn took the money, but he did not hold up his end of the bargain. Instead, he and his men hunkered down for the winter in the marshes around Lincolnshire. By avoiding any direct contact against William's forces, the Danish did not suffer the same fate as the Anglo-Saxons did around York.

However, they were affected by William's scorched-earth policy. By the time winter ended in early 1070, the Vikings who had remained were starving and weakened after the cold winter. Their spirits were soon lifted as King Sweyn II arrived with reinforcements. An initial assessment of the remaining forces likely caused him to abandon any idea of a full-scale invasion, though. Instead, he opted to conduct the typical raids. During this time, he encountered Hereward the Wake, an Anglo-Saxon who had lost everything to the Normans and now lived on a small island called Ely. Hereward's exploits were recorded, and they captured the imagination of people over the next couple of centuries. Over time, his life would become a tale of a man seeking to reclaim the lands that were taken from him. This shows that even long after the Norman established themselves, some resentment lingered after the king had died.

Together, the King Sweyn II and Hereward the Wake began a march against Peterborough. The *Anglo-Saxon Chronicle* claims that they targeted Peterborough because William I was going to appoint a new abbot there. During May and June of 1070, they sacked the abbey, where the Norman Turold of Fécamp was to become abbot. According to some sources, the sacking of this religious place was justified because they did not want the wealth to be taken by the Normans. This was actually a legitimate fear, as William I had been raiding other monasteries and religious facilities to pay his army. It is also possible that Hereward had wanted to use the money from the abbey to pay for his own army.

However, it was the Vikings who decided what would happen with the riches they had stolen. Claiming most of it for themselves, they decided that they did not need to remain any longer in England. After extorting more money out of William I to leave, the Danish Vikings tried to return home in 1070 CE. After breaking the alliance with Hereward and absconding with most of the wealth, the Vikings found that karma was not too far behind them. Most of the ships and the majority of the booty they had taken over the year were sunk as they made their way back to the continent.

The loss of his Viking allies did not seem to deter Hereward from his goal, which is likely why he gained such a prominent place in the stories passed down after his death. Determined to be a thorn in William's side, he would successfully establish a base for his rebels at Ely Abbey. The subsequent guerrilla campaigns against the Normans attracted the attention of other Anglo-Saxon rebels. When 1071 began, the small contingent of Anglo-Saxon rebels that were left after the Vikings deserted them had grown to a much larger threat, which included three other notable leaders: Æthelwine (once the bishop of Durham), Morcar (once the earl of Northumbria), and Waltheof (a powerful noble of Northumbria).

William had sent a few expeditions against them, but it became clear that they were not going to be able to quickly stifle the growing rebellion as they had during the winter of 1069, and so, William marched north to face them.

He sent men through two different routes to lay siege to the abbey where the rebels were staying. Upon seeing the sturdy structure made of stone, William knew that siege equipment would be necessary to properly drive the men from hiding. Getting his army to the abbey had been difficult enough, but he sent for the equipment because he did not want to leave anything to chance.

The Anglo-Saxons saw how William was planning to attack, and knowing that they could not win under siege, they slipped away before William's siege could even begin. Without needing to initiate any actual fighting, William I had managed to win the battle, largely based on his reputation. By this point, his military prowess was well known around the island.

Those who had not managed to escape would face William's reputation and his brutal nature. Captured rebels were often blinded or mutilated, while others were placed in prison for the rest of their lives. Both Æthelwine and Morcar suffered cruel fates, though Morcar would survive and be released after outliving the Norman king. Waltheof, who became the earl of Northumbria in 1072, had a complicated relationship with the king, and this was not the first time where he had caused problems. However, William had ended up settling with the earl. Bizarrely enough, the king ended up giving his niece, Judith of Lens, to the earl in marriage. Waltheof is said to have been one of the last Anglo-Saxon earls, and he was executed under William's orders in 1076. Hereward managed to escape with some of his men, living to continue the rebellion elsewhere.

The actual fate of Hereward is unknown, though, as different sources provided different fates for the man. Some say that he was eventually killed by Norman soldiers. Others claim that he made peace with the king, with little details on exactly what kind of peace they were able to find, given how they both felt wronged by the other. Finally, some sources say that Hereward left the island entirely, living out the rest of his years on the continent.

Beyond the Rebellious Northern Anglo-Saxons

It appeared that William had finally gotten most of the north under his control, though it took him five long years to do so. However, he would soon find that the Anglo-Saxons who had resisted him had been a bit of a buffer to another long-standing enemy of the English—the Scottish.

Following the Norman conquest, the Scots had begun to allow the Anglo-Saxon rebels to live in the upper part of the island. King Malcolm III had been quick to find a way to continue to cause problems for whatever king was on the English throne by aiding and abetting his enemies. Military support was offered to the English rebels, particularly Edgar Ætheling. The king had married Edward the Confessor's niece (Edgar's sister), Margaret, giving him more of a stake in fighting against the

Normans.

The Scots would constantly raid the area of Northumbria, but until 1072, William had not had a chance to face the Scottish king. It was all he could do to fight the forces to the south and the immediate north. With all of his other enemies finally out of the way, he turned his attention to the Scots. He was successful in stopping the raids and forcing Malcolm III to negotiate a peace agreement. As a part of that agreement, Edgar Ætheling (the man with the best claim to the throne) was forced into exile, spending the rest of his life in Flanders.

Atoning for the Conquest

Though he had managed to conquer the English, it is thought that William I felt some regret or that he at least desired to atone for what had happened that day at Hastings. Many men on both sides lost their lives over the course of the day. Around 1071, he had commissioned the construction of an abbey where the battle had been. It would seem that William I also had some respect for the king he had killed as he had ordered that the abbey's high altar be placed on the location where Harold II's body had been found after the battle had ended.

It is no longer scattered and stained with the bones and blood of those who fought in it, but the memories of the horrors of that day have lived until today, and it remains as one of the most well-known battles of the Middle Ages.

Though William had been successful in finally conquering the island, it had come at a high cost, both in money and in lives. It is unlikely that William had anticipated nearly as much resistance as he had faced, and his military prowess was tested in a way that it never would have been tested on the continent because of the strange island dynamics. The Battle of Hastings was likely the only time where William I could have been defeated, as Harold II was the only man with the experience and following that could have stopped him. Once William had defeated the king, it was mostly a matter of time before the rest of England would come under his reign.

Chapter 11 – The Domesday Book

William I spent about five years fighting a range of enemies. Between fighting the longtime enemies of the English and the English rebels who would not accept him, William spent a considerable amount of money ensuring that he had the army required to protect his claim as king. While he was willing to raid religious establishments, as well as taking from the Anglo-Saxon nobles to give to the Normans and others who had supported him during the initial invasion, this was not a sustainable method of funding an entire kingdom.

Toward the end of his reign, William I knew that he needed to set up a tax system to ensure that the Anglo-Saxons did not rise up and remove his lineage the way they had removed the Viking usurpers. The result was the Domesday Book.

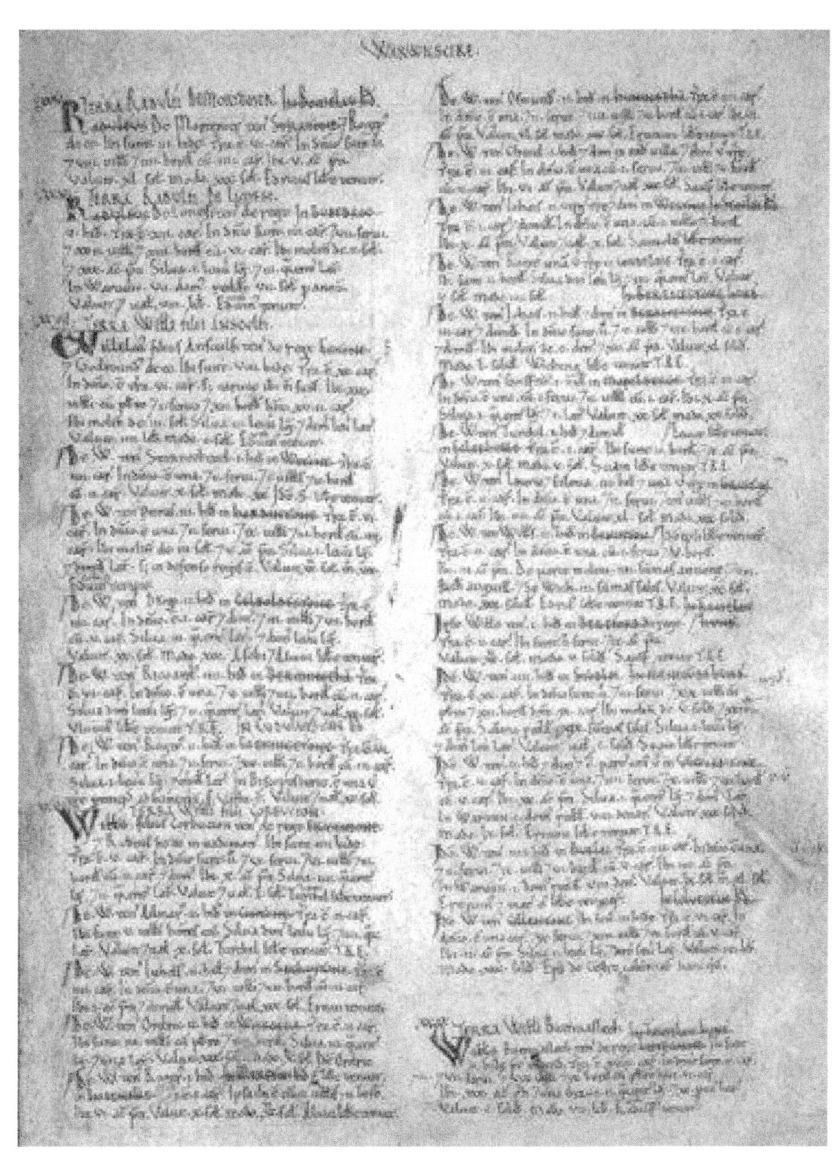

Page from the Domesday Book
https://commons.wikimedia.org/wiki/File:Domesday_book--w.jpg

Commission of the Domesday Book

William's method of determining tax rates for his kingdom was based on a series of surveys that he commissioned in December of 1085. With nearly two decades between the time of his conquest and the time when he commissioned the survey, there was a question of which parts of the kingdom had recovered from his early methods to stamp out rebellions and which locations had prospered the most from his reign. The surveys were to result in a record of the status of the different regions, including both the cash and property wealth of his subjects.

Initial Assessment

Some data existed from earlier assessments, but there was no complete record of the status of each of the different regions. Since William had been so brutal in putting down rebellions, any records from before his conquest were likely obsolete anyway.

Royal commissioners were appointed to manage the surveys of the entire kingdom. At the time, the English counties stretched from the southern parts of the island to the Scottish border, which was at the Rivers Tees and Ribble. The commissioners were sent to the seven different regions, with three or four commissioners going to each region, and they were given a series of questions to ask the overlords and their subjects. Each county was to pick representatives who could speak to the status of the county and its assets.

According to the first account of the wealth of the different realms in William's kingdom, the commissioners identified 13,418 settlements. Each of the settlements, as determined by the commissioners, were compared to records that had been recorded earlier (both before the Norman conquest and since William's coronation). The findings were then entered in, giving a complete account of the wealth of those different counties. As was normal during the Middles Ages, the language used for official information like this was Latin, so the commissioners entered their data in a language that would likely be much easier for people to read today than if they had written it in Old English (Latin had not evolved since it was a dead language by the 11th century —it had become many different Italian dialects by this point). The Domesday Book was published in 1086, and it still exists today, though it is no longer updated now.

While it was meant as a way of determining the taxes of the region, what the Domesday Book does today is provide a unique look into the many different aspects of the kingdom that we would not have ordinarily gotten. The use of the lands was different across the kingdom, as well as the disputes that were currently causing problems for the landowners and their people. It provides a look at the lives of the people of the kingdom, something that is not available in nearly any other kingdom of the Middle Ages. For example, looking at the book today shows us what the most common means of raising money were in each of the districts and how much would have to be sold to pay the taxes levied on those areas.

Another interesting aspect that can be gleaned from the Domesday Book is that by the end of William I's reign, only four major English landowners had retained power. It is possible that William may have retained more of them had they not rebelled against him in the first five years. While he was certain to give away Anglo-Saxon lands to satisfy those who had supported his venture, many of the Anglo-Saxon nobles had perished at the Battle of Hastings. So, it is possible that he would not have had to take many lands from the remaining noble families. However, they proved to be difficult or flat-out refused to recognize his claim. Ultimately, William had to bring in more people from the continent to help him manage the kingdom. Men like Waltheof were few, and twenty years after the conquest, the Anglo-Saxon rulers were almost entirely removed from power, as shown by the Domesday Book.

Following its publication, many of those who reviewed the contents of the book felt that it was beyond what could have been expected, particularly given the number of lands and how diverse the means of making money were at the time. One person quipped that "there was no single hide nor a yard of land, nor indeed one ox nor one cow nor one pig which was left out." The lengthy account of the affairs, assets, and wealth of the settlements across the kingdom soon began to be compared with the Christian Last Judgment, which states that all Christian lives would be accounted for and judged upon their death. About one hundred years later, this comparison would result in the book being called the Domesday Book as a reference to the Last Judgment.

Despite the name, the records actually required two books to cover all of the data collected by the commissioners. The first volume is known as the Great Domesday, and it has data on all but three counties in the kingdom of 1086. The three absent counties are Essex, Norfolk, and Suffolk, which are included in the second volume, commonly referred to as the Little Domesday. It is unknown why these three counties were not summarized and added to the larger book. Combined, the books are 413 pages long, giving historians today an unprecedented look at the lives and state of the kingdom over nine centuries ago.

Chapter 12 – Effects of the Conquest

While the majority of the landowners and people controlling the regions may have been largely Norman, the people themselves were not replaced. England continued to be structured based on the traditions of the people. Over time, William I and the kings who followed him would begin to change that structure. Some people are under the impression that William I immediately implemented the changes, but it is far more likely that the changes to the different English systems were gradual. William I may not have learned much about the people that he believed he was promised to rule prior to Edward's death, but he did not appear to have intended to recreate Normandy in England. Given the problems that he had with the French king before his death, William may have seen the new lands as a way to start a kingdom according to his own methods. Remember, he had inherited Normandy as the bastard son of the previous lord, and he had become the new lord when he was still young. He had learned how to rule based on what others had established because of how young he was when he was placed in control.

While William was considerably different than previous kings (both Anglo-Saxon and Viking), he did take a greater interest in uniting the nation in a way that it had not been united in a long time. After all, his reign was preceded by questions of who the next rightful heir would be. The Vikings had continually taken control of the kingdom from the Anglo-Saxon over a century or so. Unlike William, though, they really had not replaced the people in charge, but they had reduced the influence of the prominent families or drove them into exile. Edward himself had been a victim of the constant changes in the crown, as he had spent most of his childhood and early adulthood in Normandy. William would finally give the nation of England a steady line of rulers with a more uniform method of ruling the people.

Changes to the Buildings and Records

One of the most obvious changes (looking at the structures built prior to the Norman conquest) is the building of structures, which were very different from what had existed on the island prior to William's arrival. The most notable change was in the number of castles that were built following the conquest. For the most part, Anglo-Saxons did not build castles, so there are few structures that could be classified as castles prior to 1066.

Initially, castles were made of wood, but the Normans soon began to build the more familiar stone castles that now dot much of the landscapes today. If you visit the United Kingdom today, many of the castle tours that you can take are only possible because of the events of October 14th, 1066.

In addition to the castles, William began to have cathedrals and abbeys improved and rebuilt to be larger. During this time, the architecture that was common across continental Europe began to appear across England.

Even the churches attended by the common people often saw changes to make them more fashionable, at least according to the continental idea of fashion.

For all of the changes that were made under William, particularly architecture and law, it is thought that William I was likely illiterate, or that if he could read, he was not adept at it. Most of his life had been spent fighting for lands that were either rightfully his (as Normandy was after his father's death) or that he believed to be rightfully his. Because of these hardships, he had learned the importance of having records of events, whether they were land assessments or battles. This was one of the major reasons why there are so many records of his reign and how much the island nation had changed after the arrival of the Normans. That does not mean that the Anglo-Saxons did not keep records. We have their side of the story because of the annals they kept. However, they were not as rigorous in recording histories, as seen by the large gaps in events. The Normans made sure to write down nearly everything they thought was important, and that included how the government was to be run in the kingdom.

Old English was largely spoken by the people, while the Norman nobles largely spoke French. However, all government business was conducted and written in Latin, as seen in the Domesday Book. English and French were two drastically different languages, which made it difficult to communicate between the different classes. Latin was the one language that anyone who had any power or education would know. Even many of the common people would know basic Latin because it was used by priests during mass. As a language that was best understood by a majority of the people, Latin became the official language of the government. This still holds true today in English-speaking countries; their legal terms are all Latin, and many English-speaking nations use Latin in their governments (though principal documents are now written in English so that they can be understood by everyone, such as portions of the Magna Carta and the American Declaration of Independence and the US Constitution).

As seen with the creation of the Domesday Book, William I raised taxes on his people. By this point, most of the men in power were loyal to him, perhaps making this an easier action to take than it would have been had the Anglo-Saxon earls still been in power. The Norman lords had less land, which meant that their taxes were not as great as they would have been under the old division of the lands. However, it still was not a popular move. The king may not have faced rebellions because of the new taxes, but he did have some who resisted or lied to get out of paying as many taxes as they should have owed. The rise in taxes was easily justified as the first five years of constant rebellions and attacks from outsiders had been a huge strain on the Normans. William I's military strategies saw them eventually subdue their enemies, but to ensure that he could remain effective, he needed to have money, as well as loyalty. They still did not have a standing army, so William needed to be able to offer money to persuade people to leave their lands alone or to hire mercenaries when problems arose.

It is interesting to note that it was during this time that royal forests were first introduced. William I established royal forests, and they were ruled by their own set of laws. Perhaps the easiest correlation is how those forests would evolve by the time of Kings Richard I and John and the tales of Robin Hood. Only the nobility was allowed to hunt on these lands unless authorization was given to others to join them. It was just one more way to mark the difference between those in power and those who were not.

One tradition that the Normans brought with them from the continent was the idea of trial by battle. Problems between people of equal standing used to be settled through courts and negotiations. Under the Norman systems, a person in the higher classes of society could face an accuser in a trial by combat in order to determine who was in the right. In theory, the Christian god would settle the dispute because he would be on the side of the person who was right. Over time, trial by combat would lose some of the gravitas that it had when it was done as a way to settle legal disputes, as it instead became a way for people to settle pettier differences. These trials would devolve into duels over time.

Changes to the Elite, Society, and the Church

Because of the number of people who had chosen to fight the invaders than to submit to them, the change in power went well beyond just the people who were beside the king in his court. The changes also extended beyond just those who managed the different counties as well. Government officials were largely changed so that William knew he could trust them. This is likely why it was so easy for the changes to take effect more quickly than they otherwise would have.

The Church also saw a huge shift as the Anglo-Saxon church officials had largely sided with the English. Around the time of the Domesday Book's publication, only one of the fifteen bishops in the kingdom was English, while eleven were Normans. Three others had been brought in from different places around the continent.

With this change to the power dynamic in the country, the practice of giving lands in exchange for loyalty and services rendered to the king became far more common, which was a practice that was not nearly as prominent before the arrival of the Normans. Prior to William's arrival, the Anglo-Saxons had determined how much service they were required to give the king (including military aid) based on the lands that they owned. As seen with Harold Godwinson following his father's death, earls were not allowed to have too much land as it would cause an imbalance in power. Under the Norman power structure, though, a person could continue to increase their lands and power, just as William had done as a young man when he consolidated power in and around Normandy.

As a direct result of a loyal family being able to gain more lands from the king, the family dynamics began to change. Nobles were now able to gain land through inheritance and conquest, and lands could be divided among several heirs instead of them passing down to one person. This created more tension in some families, particularly as some sons were excluded, but it tightened the bonds of others.

By putting people who were loyal to him in all of the major positions of power, both secular and religious, William was able to enact changes that likely would not have been possible had he been faced with the Anglo-Saxon earls. They were accustomed to autonomy, which would have made it more difficult for William to enact these changes.

The constant rebellions by the Anglo-Saxons also meant that the earldoms were reduced in size to better ensure that problems were easier to manage. Small earldoms meant that William I could offer more lands to his loyal followers, but it also meant that the new earls would have to continue to work hard to gain more power and influence. This made the power dynamic more geared toward a hierarchy that would keep the king on top and the nobles fighting among themselves to gain power and influence (instead of directly challenging the king).

The Domesday Book helped to show just how much contention there was among the people, so it was clear that a different type of court system was needed for the Normans. Called the Lords, the new courts were held by the lords of the respective lands. This began an integration of the continental feudal system in Britain because the lords of different lands would determine how a dispute would be settled. This also brought an interesting change to how a murder was resolved. The Normans reintroduced murdrum fines, which the Danes had originally introduced. These fines only applied if a Norman descendant was murdered. Should the killer fail to be identified, then the entire English community would be required to pay a fine to compensate the Norman family for the murder of their family member. While this clearly shows just how much opposition the Normans faced in the early days of William's reign, it set up a dynamic that would become incredibly problematic over the centuries. Even after the lines of inheritance were established and the difference between the Normans and the Anglo-Saxons shrunk, more importance was placed on the life of the people in power.

With an emphasis on the people in power and a shift in how lands were divided among them, the number of people who were free decreased. People who had worked the lands for themselves under the Anglo-Saxon system opted to work the lands of landlords because it was easier to be under their rule than to try to survive as they had under the old system.

William I is not generally thought of as a pious man today, but there was a marked increase in the number of monasteries in England during his reign. It is certainly an interesting dichotomy since he would also raid them for funds to keep his military funded when needed. Perhaps it was out of a sense of guilt for these transgressions that he increased the number of religious facilities. As he took lands from the Anglo-Saxons and shrunk the amount of land he gave to his loyal subjects, William kept some of the lands separate. These lands he gave to the continental monasteries, which resulted in more of them being built. It is also possible that he was trying to curry favor with the pope, who had sided with him and his claim to the English throne.

Changes in Relationships with the Continent

The Anglo-Saxons had a long and contentious relationship with the Vikings, but they had much tighter bonds with them as well. England and France did not have as deep a connection, despite the number of English nobles who fled to Normandy following the Viking conquests. However, with the Normans taking over the largest kingdom on the island, the ties that had largely bound the British and the Scandinavian countries were largely severed. Instead of the close, familial relationships that they had maintained, with many British and Scandinavian elite marrying, the bonds would be forged with the French elite instead. There would never again be a serious threat of the Scandinavian countries trying to claim the English crown.

Ironically, this would later prove to be a source of serious contention between England and France, as the claim over the French throne by an English noble would be much stronger than the claim that William I had over England. The Norman conquest is one of the reasons for both the formation of the Angevin Empire and later the Hundred Years' War, where the person with the greatest claim to the French throne was actually the English king.

A Significant Change to the Language

There are few languages that are as diverse today as they were around 1,000 years ago, but English is a notable exception. The linear evolution of most languages makes it easy to classify them as being Germanic or Romantic because the lands around the continent largely remained under the control of people who had similar languages.

England was unique in that it was under the influence of so many different languages from the time the Romans arrived. The influence of the Roman invaders can be seen in some of the older roots of the language, but most of it was removed following their departure, as the Anglo-Saxons began to resume their own traditions.

Next, the Vikings would spend several centuries raiding and then settling among the native peoples. The influence of their language is more obvious, as English is largely considered to be a Germanic language.

However, the biggest change to the English language was a direct result of the Norman invasion. Once William I became king, the primary language used by his court was the language that he spoke—French. Though it was primarily used by those of Norman descent, French was also used by some of the nobility and others of English descent, which, over time, blended with the native tongue, changing it enough that a native English speaker today cannot hope to understand the language spoken around the time of the Norman invasion.

An Interesting Note on the Norman Lineage and Previous Kings

The subjugation of the Anglo-Saxons was so complete that the Normans largely ignored the accomplishments of the kings before them. The best illustration of this desire to ignore Britain's prior history and the dubious claim of William I was in the way his descendants would look at kings who reigned before him. According to William's reasoning, he was the heir to Edward the Confessor, and without Edward's promise of the throne, William would not have had any claim that could be backed by the Normans or the Church. This should have meant that Edward would have been called King Edward I. However, he is always called simply King Edward or, more often, Edward the Confessor. This is because King Edward I was a king of Norman descent. In numbering the kings of the same name, they literally ignored the prior Anglo-Saxon king. This gave more importance to the king of Norman descent and showed a complete break between the Anglo-Saxon period and the Norman rule.

To some extent, the desire to ignore the history of the Anglo-Saxons showed an understanding on the Norman part that their claim was not legitimate. William had not come to power peacefully, and with as many years of resistance as the Normans had faced, it had to have been clear on some level to them that they were invaders, like the Vikings before them. They had just been more successful in usurping and keeping the throne. Harold II was perhaps not the rightful heir either, but his rule would not have seen a complete shift in how the kingdom was run. It is also possible that this denial of the Anglo-Saxon kings before him was in retaliation for the reception William had among his new subjects. As the English had rejected him and his claim, the Normans rejected their place in their own history.

Chapter 13 – Records of 1066 CE – Insight into a Time of Turmoil

While there is little known about most events 950 years ago, historians have a surprising amount of information about the events of 1066. It was certainly a turning point in history, but it would be expected that there would be far more of a one-sided account of what exactly happened. Instead, we have a fairly lengthy record of the events from both the Norman side and the Anglo-Saxon side. This is in large part because the Anglo-Saxons still constituted a majority of the population. The Normans may have started to claim the higher positions in government, but the Anglo-Saxons already had their own means of recording the events of their time.

The Bayeux Tapestry

The Norman version of events, including William's claim to the throne, is recorded on a 230-foot-long piece of cloth called the Bayeux Tapestry. In total, there are 75 scenes depicted on the tapestry, though it was originally longer. The end of this unique piece of art has been missing, though it is not known when this part of the tapestry was removed or why it was removed. It has led to some interesting discussions among academics about what part of history was exactly lost. We may not be able to say for certain what the last scenes were, but many people believe that it was likely a depiction of William being crowned as the new king.

The name Bayeux Tapestry is not strictly accurate as the images were not woven into the cloth, which is how tapestries are made. Instead, the scenes were embroidered onto a long piece of linen. It is estimated that the work was completed in 1070. Since it was made by the generation after the defeat of the English, it is considered to be a fairly reliable account of how the Normans viewed the events leading up to the battle. It is also believed that the Bishop of Bayeux, Odo, William's half-brother, was the one who commissioned the work. If this is true, it almost certainly depicts the events as William would have seen them, as Odo would have heard William's perspective. However, it is also possible that it has a slant because of a desire to strengthen the family's claim to the throne.

It is unfortunate that we don't know who completed this impressive needlework, as the person or persons who were the artists behind it was not recorded. It was the Anglo-Saxons who were considered the most adept at needlework in Europe, which meant that the artists were very likely Anglo-Saxons. Some speculate that the scenes depicted on the cloth were actually recorded from depictions that were in manuscripts that were located in Canterbury at the time.

The cloth reads like a book, starting on the left side and moving to the right. There are many scenes that appear to be inspired by the methods of recording histories on scrolls. This presents the events in more of a historical context, like a record instead of simply as a work of art. However, given the subject matter (the history of events leading up to the

Battle of Hastings), it provides a record of more than just the main events leading up to the battle. In this sense, it is comparable more to a work of fiction or myth since it gives the viewer a look into the details of daily life as they take in the events beings depicted.

The Bayeux Tapestry provides a lot more than just a look at the events that resulted in the Norman conquest of England. With 75 scenes, it provides a lot of context about the lives of the Norman people during the 11th century, or at least the lives of the nobles and their servants. Some scenes that might appear mundane are included, such as large dinners, the types of food they ate, and how they dressed (including servants). It goes on to depict a war council as they plan for how they will attack. There are also depictions of the way they prepared for the war. These scenes provide some hints as to what they wore when they went into battle as well. The tactics used by William the Conqueror highlight his use of the cavalry to scatter Harold II's infantry. Based on this, some think that the Normans were accustomed to using cavalry during battle and that much of their success could have come from their skill on horseback.

The cloth may be an elegant depiction of the Norman perspective, but it was most likely created by Anglo-Saxon artisans. This makes it one of the first examples of Anglo-Norman art, which would evolve over the next few decades.

Scene from the Bayeux Tapestry: William of Normandy Learns about King Edward's Death and Harold II's Coronation

Urban, Attribution-ShareAlike 3.0 Unported (CC BY-SA 3.0) https://creativecommons.org/licenses/by-sa/3.0/deed.en via Wikimedia Commons,https://commons.wikimedia.org/wiki/File:Tapisserie_agriculture.JPG

The *Anglo-Saxon Chronicle*

The *Anglo-Saxon Chronicle* is a recording of several centuries of British history, starting from the reign of King Alfred the Great in 871 CE and ending around 1154 CE, nearly a century after the Norman invasion. Unlike the Bayeux Tapestry, the chronicles are multiple works of writing. It is unknown how many have been written, but six manuscripts remain intact today. A seventh managed to survive to the modern period, but it was destroyed sometime during the 18th century.

The remaining manuscripts are designated by letters, with A being the oldest manuscript. Each copy of the manuscripts was stored in separate locations, so they do not contain all of the same information, but there is a lot of overlap in what they detail. Naturally, all of the manuscripts are recorded in Old English or Anglo-Saxon, which makes them totally inaccessible to modern-day English speakers.

Around the time of the Norman conquest, the English language began to significantly change as Normans began to integrate with the Anglo-Saxons over time. One of the manuscripts was also translated into Latin, making it more accessible to people over the years.

These chronicles are the oldest recording of any European country written in a native tongue instead of in Latin. With several hundred years recorded in these manuscripts, there are many notable events that signaled important changes on the island over the years. The Battle of Hastings is described and notes how King Harold II fought bravely despite the obvious disadvantages. It is through the *Anglo-Saxon Chronicle* that we know that Harold and two of his loyal brothers were killed that day.

All of the information recorded on the manuscripts that still survive today provides a unique look at history that is not available in nearly any other country. We are able to see several different perspectives because no single manuscript was written by just one person. They do provide biased versions of events, but they are from an angle that is more from the common person's point of view (or at least the clerics who would have tended the common people). Like the Bayeux Tapestry, the *Anglo-Saxon Chronicle* offers a look into more than just a single event, as each event covered offers details surrounding it.

What is particularly interesting about the tapestry and the *Anglo-Saxon Chronicle* is that the information they provide is reflected in each other. This is perhaps why the battle is still so well known today.

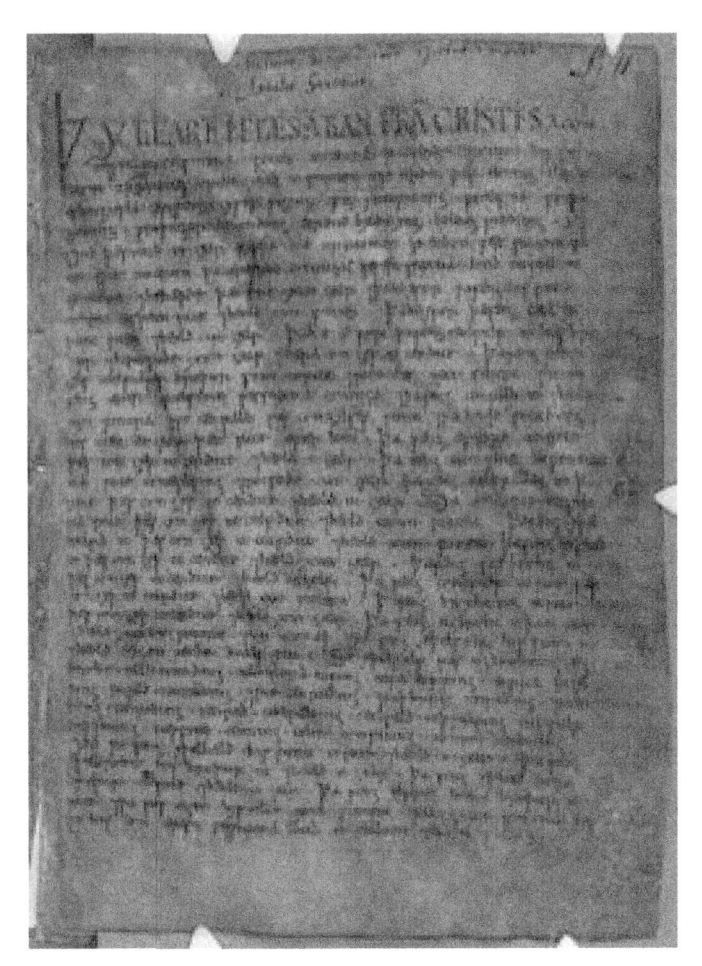

Anglo-Saxon Chronicle – Single Winchester Page of the Manuscript
https://commons.wikimedia.org/wiki/File:ASC_Parker_page.png

Conclusion

The Romans were the first recorded people to have successfully invaded the nations on the island that would one day become England, Wales, and Scotland. Not long after they left the island, the Vikings began to attack. Unlike the Romans, the Vikings would largely integrate with the people of Britain. To fight the stream of Viking invaders who had no interest in turning the island into a home, the Anglo-Saxons rose up.

With the ebb and flow of power, there was a constant question of succession. The Vikings who managed to take the Anglo-Saxon throne were considered pretenders. But what really made the succession of the English throne difficult was that royalty would frequently intermarry (something that happened throughout Europe, which made the question of succession a constant problem elsewhere as well), so even if there was not a claim to the throne by blood, many rulers could claim it through marriage. The short period where the Anglo-Saxons retook the throne ended not long after King Æthelred II was restored and then suddenly died. Though he had children by his first wife, his second wife, Emma of

Normandy, was far more assertive and found a way to keep the throne by marrying King Cnut, a Viking who had invaded and claimed the throne for himself. It was from this that the question of succession would become muddled a couple of decades later. Eventually, her son, Edward, would achieve the throne (though he was not the son she had wanted to ascend it). He only achieved the crown by agreeing to the terms set by the Anglo-Saxons, particularly Godwin.

When King Edward the Confessor died without any children, the kingdom fell back into the quagmire of determining succession. As Edward had made vague promises of succession throughout most of his life, there were several people who felt they were entitled to the throne, most notably William the Bastard, the ruler of Normandy. When Harold Godwinson was quickly coronated as the new king, William felt that his throne had been stolen.

While William planned to invade, another man who felt he had a claim to the throne, King Harald Hardrada of Norway, attacked in the north. King Harold II had no sooner defeated him than William arrived in the south. The Battle of Hastings would see the death of King Harold and the end of the Anglo-Saxon period.

William the Bastard became known as William the Conqueror, and under his reign, England began to change. From the social structure and the way the government ran to the language itself, the island nation began to more closely resemble the continental countries.

Though William ultimately became king, two very different accounts of the events leading up to the Battle of Hastings have come down through the ages: the Bayeux Tapestry and the *Anglo-Saxon Chronicle*. It gives historians a better look at the factions and ideas of the conqueror and the conquered, something that we seldom get to see following a successful invasion of any nation or kingdom. This has made it easier to get a more well-rounded understanding of the different perspectives and shows a historic transition of a nation that would one day be one of the largest empires in the world.

Part 2: William the Conqueror

A Captivating Guide to the First Norman King of England Who Defeated the English Army Led by the King of the Anglo-Saxons in the Battle of Hastings

Introduction

In Bayeux, a city located in modern-day northern France, the local priests possessed a tapestry that was over 230 feet (70 meters) long and 20 inches (50 centimeters) tall. This gigantic tapestry had a tale embroidered onto it, a tale of how the Normans had invaded England, how the English king had died, and how the Norman duke had succeeded him to the throne. It's a tale that would go down in history, written down by numerous contemporaries with various perspectives, a tale that would inspire some while fascinate and even terrify others. It's a tale of a man from a seemingly small land rising to rule one of the most powerful, stable kingdoms in all of Europe at the time, a kingdom that would sow the seeds of an empire that would sprout many centuries later. The native Normans (and the modern French) would know him as *Guillaume le Conquérant*, but to the English-speaking world, he is known and revered as William the Conqueror.

William's story is a fascinating yarn full of twists and turns, wins and losses, political intrigue, and good, old-fashioned raw bursts of emotion.

Summing it up is always difficult, especially considering the naming conventions and the revolving door of titles, both political and ecclesiastical. Going over this book, the reader will come across dozens, if not hundreds, of people with the same name, be it Roger, Ralph, Robert, Odo/Eudo, Henry, Richard, Edward, Cnut, Harold/Harald, Edith, or, of course, William. Throughout the years, battles would be fought over and over in the same locations, and subjects would be loyal, then rebel, then put in chains, then pardoned, then rebel again, and so on *ad infinitum.*

So, what is the best way to tell the story of one of the most important political figures in medieval western Europe in a summarized, easy-to-digest format? Well, there's no easy answer there, mainly because William's life is filled to the brim with events and individuals that, truth be told, deserve books upon books of their own. This particular book will try to cover the most important aspects of his life, from his coronation to his exploits in Normandy, the famed Battle of Hastings in 1066, his years as a king, the creation of the Domesday Book, and the impact he made on the world. So many various details will simply have to be left out, like his extensive church activities or handpicked legal and ducal dealings with the common folk. In that sense, and that sense alone, this book is not a comprehensive look at William's life; rather, it is an expanded summation of what made him the man he was and the inspiration he still remains to millions of people worldwide.

In some ways, William's life is quite in line with the mores of his time; he would often be no different than any other medieval ruler, be they the Holy Roman emperor, the Angevine count, the Hungarian king, or the prince of Kievan Rus. But once you delve deeper into the events that occurred during the Norman king's life, you'll see just how innovative, atypical, and, for lack of a better term, different William was. From his birth at Falaise to his death at Rouen, he has been through everything that medieval Europe could throw at him, and, as is evident from hundreds of thousands of books on the subject, including this one, he stood the test of time and achieved proverbial immortality.

Statue of William the Conqueror in Falaise, France
https://commons.wikimedia.org/wiki/File:Statue_d%27Dgilliaume_l%C3%A9_Contch%C3%A9tha nt_%C3%A0_Falaise_01.jpg

Chapter 1 – William's Early Days: Birth, Childhood, Adolescence, and Early Reign over the Normans

"William the Bastard" Is Born

William was born in either 1027 or 1028 at the Falaise castle. He was the son of Duke Robert I, who would later be known as Robert the Magnificent. Robert came to power after the sudden death of his older brother, Duke Richard III. The duke's death was recorded to be August 6th, 1027, and considering how strained the relations between the two brothers were, some contemporary sources claimed that Robert had somehow been involved with Richard's death in order to reach dukedom. Modern scholars find this to be unlikely, but the idea does sound plausible; fratricide and political intrigue were definitely a huge part of the medieval court life in both France and Normandy. Taking the date of Robert's ascension into account, we can assume that William was either conceived soon after the coronation or that his mother was, at the very least, already carrying him. Once again, modern science and history don't have the exact date, but the most common consensus is late 1028, when Robert was a well-established duke and a new status quo was already in place.

Robert's own life, as well as that of his ancestors, is an interesting study, which we will cover in a bit, but the most intriguing part about William's conception is, in fact, not related to his father but to his mother. According to most recorded medieval sources, his mother was a woman by the name of Herleva. Medieval authors disagree on the exact vocation of her father, a certain Fulbert. He was either a tanner, an embalmer, an apothecary, a furrier, an individual who would lay out corpses ready for funerals, a minor member of the burgher class, or even the chamberlain of the duke. More than likely, Fulbert (and, by extension, Herleva) was a commoner from the ministerial class who lived in Falaise.

The fact that Herleva was a commoner, in addition to her not being mentioned as Duke Robert I's wife, quite strongly suggests that William's conception was out of wedlock, making him an illegitimate son of Robert, i.e., a bastard. Ever since antiquity, bastardy was seen as an important element that can delegitimize an heir. The practice became especially prominent with the advent of Christianity, considering how important marriage as an institution (both political and religious) was to the Church.

However, the problem with William being "a bastard" is the fact that, in medieval times, there were dozens of caveats that circumvented Christian dogma and allowed anyone to take the throne, despite their birth. For example, divorce or a marriage annulment were viewed to be just as anti-Christian as having children out of wedlock. However, there are dozens upon dozens of records in Rome of prominent bishops allowing annulments and blessing new marriages (often those of political convenience). The reasons behind these acts are manifold, and they usually include either a close friendship or familial kinship between the priests and ruling families, desperate acts that would save the bishopric from the local ruler's wrath, or even earning political favors for the local parishes. In fact, one of the reasons why younger siblings in royal houses would take up monastic vows is precisely so that their family could have a secure foothold in the Church and earn political and religious favors later in life. The Great Schism between Constantinople and Rome would occur during William's lifetime, and the Eastern Church was no different in that regard. Medieval rulers would be allowed to marry and divorce three times, and even though there are plenty of examples of rulers taking up a fourth wife, the Church would almost always show leniency. In other words, the Church could legitimize anyone if it felt they would obey the word of God and, more importantly, invest time and money in the Church itself. The same applied to illegitimate sons of rulers; medieval Wallachia, for instance, is full of dukes and princes (called "voivodes" in Romanian) who were bastards. More to the point, most of these rulers couldn't even prove their lineage to the former voivode himself, meaning that, technically, you could simply announce that your father was a prominent ruler, and you would be a viable candidate for the throne.

However, even if we took all of that into account, as well as every single Church canon as set in stone and unyielding, William would still not technically be a bastard. Herleva, though a woman of humble birth, was, in an official capacity, Robert's concubine. In contemporary Normandy, rulers could take up any number of concubines alongside their lawful wives. In fact, Robert's grandfather, Richard I, who was first the count and then the duke of Normandy, ruling from 942 to 996, had a concubine named Gunnor, whom he later married. Her own son was Richard II, the man who would succeed Richard I as the duke of Normandy and father both Richard III and Robert I. During the time of Richard I, Christianity and Christian norms were extolled by the Norman aristocracy, despite the prominent practice of keeping concubines. Moreover, children who were descendants from concubines would often hold high positions in society, either as landowners, minor lords, or members of the clergy. Despite the practice of keeping concubines, Norman dukes were seen as model Christians, and their sons would succeed their fathers with little to no legal issues. And to really hammer this point home, it wasn't just the Normans who kept concubines at court. There were rulers all across France who did the exact same thing, and bastardy was not seen as a major issue there either.

Finally, we don't have any sources contemporary to William's birth that would suggest the Church's disapproval of William as a legitimate heir to Robert's throne. In fact, based on what little information we do have, it's more than likely that the members of the elites saw William as a legal successor from the very day he was born.

So, why did the moniker "William the Bastard" stick? Well, it all comes down to the circumstances of the medieval authors who first called William by that name. Nearly all the official sources that talk about William's early life were written at least a few decades after his death. Considering his accomplishments at the time, as well as the Church's views on wars of conquest, killing, and other crimes, both actual and supposed, the view of William was extremely critical, to the point where medieval authors would exaggerate, overemphasize, or even outright invent parts of his life. Whether or not a priest was sympathetic to William's cause, he had to look at the situation from the perspective of a godly man, to whom Christian virtues outweighed any practicalities of running a country. These practices would become even more one-sided if the priest disliked a ruler, so it wasn't uncommon for dukes and kings like William to be outright demonized.

In short, at least to his contemporaries, both during his childhood and throughout his life, William was not viewed as a bastard. He was as legitimate as any duke of Normandy before and after him.

At this point, it would be instructive to take a look at William's parents, Duke Robert and Herleva, in some detail. Their relationship, both politically and interpersonally speaking, might be one of the main factors that shaped young William's world view and future aspirations as a ruler.

Robert, as stated above, came into power after the short reign of his brother, Duke Richard III, a reign that saw the brothers wage war and that saw Richard die a sudden death, which some sources at the time readily attributed to foul play on Robert's part. In addition, there was a third brother, who had the monastic name Nicholas, and it was assumed that Robert forced this brother to take monastic vows so that he wouldn't be a threat to the Norman throne. Even if that were the case, Nicholas seemed to have accepted this new life, becoming an oblate at the abbey of Fécamp (the birthplace of Robert's father, as well as other immediate ancestors) and later an abbot at Saint-Ouen of Rouen in 1042. Interestingly, he was the only Norman abbot who contributed to William's ships during his 1066 expedition to England.

Just like the question of William's supposed bastardy, the question of his father's propensity for cruel acts was an exaggeration by the medieval authors who penned the books on William's parents. By all accounts, Robert behaved no differently than any other Norman ruler in early 11th century Normandy. At the time, the region was a collection of territories held by local dukes and princes, all vying for power and supremacy over each other, and who were all under some influence from the French court. For instance, Falaise, the place where William was born, was close to Argentan, which itself was close to the very contested frontier zone. Farther south was the town of Sées, which was controlled by the Bellême family, but whose church was under the jurisdiction of the archbishops of Rouen. Sées was far from being the only area in Normandy to have such a complicated political situation, but at the time of Robert's ascension to the throne, it was one of the most difficult to handle.

Robert saw some political and military successes before 1035, as he managed to consolidate power south beyond Argentan and west to the borders of Brittany. In northeastern Normandy, Robert married one of his sisters to Count Baldwin IV, a ruler who held dominion over Flanders. This marriage was especially important since it provided Robert with a powerful ally in times of need. Robert himself had sent troops to assist both Count Baldwin and the new king of France at the time, Henry I. Speaking of King Henry, Robert had been such a prominent ally of his that he was present at the Royal Court on April 1st, 1032, on Easter, among other powerful princes and dukes. Robert proved himself to be a supporter of Henry during the French king's conflict with his mother Constance, who wanted to depose Henry and replace him with his brother, also named Robert.

In the 1030s, Robert waged wars to preserve Norman influence over the lands close to the border. Powerful players, such as Count Fulk Nerra of Anjou, his son Count Geoffrey Martel, and Count Odo II of Blois-Chartres, all had expansionist policies, with Nerra, in particular, desiring to dominate the county of Maine, as well as the areas south Robert's dukedom's borders. One common element that all Norman rulers exhibited at the time, including William's father and grandfather, was the frequent use of anger and violence to achieve stability. One anecdote speaks of Fulk Nerra kicking his son while he lay prostrate on the floor, begging for forgiveness after staging a failed rebellion. Geoffrey Martel supposedly had to carry a saddle on his shoulders and walk several miles in shame. William was, of course, well acquainted with these types of behavior, both from his father's court and from the other prominent rulers of the time. This tactic of using anger as a political decision-making and decision-enforcing tool would be one that William would frequently use throughout his own reign.

However, anger and violence were not the only aspects of ruling that William would be influenced by. In his later years, Duke Robert showed signs of wanting to abandon his past "bad behavior" and seek atonement for his sins by playing a more prominent role in Church affairs. He founded two major religious houses, a nunnery north of the river Seine at Montivilliers and a monastery at Cerisy in western Normandy. Robert was also present when the relics of Saint Nicaise were transferred, along with other saints, to Saint-Ouen of Rouen on December 12th, 1032. William would have grown up in an atmosphere where the atonement for one's sins and reliance on the Church were at their peak in terms of political relevance.

Unlike Duke Robert, Herleva is someone history knows precious little about. As stated, her origins are not exactly known, and her father was, in all likelihood, a member of the ministerial class—in other words, a commoner. It was not uncommon for the dukes to recruit servants from this particular segment of society, so both Fulbert and Herleva playing a role in court, no matter how minor, is quite plausible. Had Fulbert been elected as chamberlain to Robert, it would have made both him and his daughter privy to some of the duke's private affairs. More importantly, the young duke would definitely have "open access" to Herleva as either a concubine or a wife.

Relations between Robert and Herleva actually endured for almost ten years. Despite her status as a concubine, circumstantial evidence suggests that Robert definitely held her in high regard. For instance, even when he had gone through a short and fruitless marriage with Estrith, the sister of

Cnut, who was the king of England, Denmark, and Norway by 1028, Robert did not force Herleva out of the court.

Depending on the sources, Herleva married another noble either shortly before or shortly after Robert's death in 1035. This man was named Herluin, and he was a minor lord of Conteville. The couple would end up having two sons, who would become massively important during William's reign, as well as two daughters. Herluin was an important part of Robert's court, acting as a lord who protected the coast of the south bank of the river Seine's estuary; a nearby canal called *Fossa Herluini* was even named after him.

William's close bond with his stepbrothers later in his life, as well as the fact that William acted cruelly a few times after Herleva's heritage was mocked, shows that he developed genuine feelings of love and admiration for his mother. In other words, to William, the question of his ancestry was definitely an important issue and a sensitive topic. However, his behavior does not hint, even once, that he acted this way to escape the label of bastardy and the shame of being born to a low-status woman. In fact, it's far more likely that he had loved his mother and that her staying at court for so long (and being involved in her son's life directly) had shaped William into being the family-oriented individual he would become later in life. Some historians argue that Robert was just as respectful of Herleva as William was, despite both of them having to remarry.

William's Castle in Falaise, France
Nitot, CC BY-SA 4.0 <https://creativecommons.org/licenses/by-sa/4.0>, via Wikimedia Commons
https://commons.wikimedia.org/wiki/File:Chateau-falaise-calvados.jpg

William's Childhood

As a child, William is mentioned at least seven times in various charters alongside his father before 1035. Norman nobles in the 11th century would often travel with their designated successors, and when a charter was being written at a monastery or any other important site, the name of the noble would be followed by those of his issue. In other words, Duke Robert must have seen young William as his legitimate successor as early as the boy's toddler years. This type of behavior is, incidentally, another indicator that shows us William was not seen as a bastard during his tender years.

During his early childhood, William had at least one named tutor, a person by the name of Ralph. The list of William's tutors would stretch all the way to his adolescence, but sadly, we don't know the intricate details of what the young Norman noble was taught. Of course, we can speculate on what he had acquired based on his behavior alone, as well as the customs in Norman lands at the time.

William was known as someone who held the written word and the Church's texts in extremely high regard. As the ruler's firstborn son, he constantly attended various meetings and events that took place in churches, so he definitely had a decent grasp of the Latin language. It's possible that he wasn't necessarily literate, as was often the case with contemporary medieval rulers, but at the very least, he could speak and understand Latin.

As an aristocrat, William had to learn the fine details of behaving like a member of the upper class, namely the ethical principles and the performative skills of rulers. Since he spent so much time with his father, and since he was at the court for the majority of his early life, the young heir must have at least picked up on the finer details of aristocratic living, even if there wasn't anyone in particular who could have taught him that.

Naturally, the future duke had to be taught the basics of fighting. Europe of the 1030s was filled with violence and near-constant warfare, and knowing how to effectively end an opponent was a normal part of a noble's curriculum. In addition to killing humans, William must have also been taught how to kill animals. Game hunting was one of the favorite pastimes of all medieval leaders, and as a child, William had to have picked up on these skills either directly from his tutors or indirectly by observing others.

Even as a young boy, the future duke of Normandy was handsome and strong for his age (at the time of Robert's death in around 1035, William was about eight or nine years old). Robert, in particular, was quite fond of young William specifically because of how healthy and strong he looked. And while we don't exactly know if William reciprocated these feelings, we can safely assume that he saw his father as a role model for a good ruler based on his behavior when he took the crown. We do, however, know that William held Herleva in high regard, and considering how prominent she was in the Norman court, it's not impossible to think that she cared about her son just as much. As odd as this might seem, William, unlike most members of the European aristocracy in the Middle Ages (and beyond), had a relatively normal childhood, with two loving parents being relatively close at all times.

Some sources from the time state that William was a loud, boisterous, and even violent child who would provoke fights with other children and often quarrel with adults. Even if we take these statements at face value (because none of them can be verified, historically speaking), this behavior is not uncommon for a young prepubescent boy, let alone a young aristocrat who was the first in line to succeed the throne. In addition, other relevant historical sources state that some of his childhood friends and cousins would grow up to be his close allies in the future. Among them were his cousin Guy of Burgundy, William Fitz Osbern, a magnate, and Duke Robert's steward, who would become one of William's closest associates in the future (he was also a distant cousin of the ruling dynasty), and one of William's half-brothers on Herleva's side, Odo, the later bishop of Bayeux and one of the most powerful people in England after William took power. As a quick aside, Bayeux Cathedral, of which Odo was made bishop by William in 1049, was the original home of the famous Bayeux Tapestry that depicts the events of William's conquest of England.

A burning question among scholars is how the contemporary aristocracy in Normandy saw William in terms of succession rights. As stated earlier, children born to concubines out of wedlock had no trouble assuming power, and the fact that William was present in so many church charters only strengthens the view that William was seen as legitimate by his immediate family. But the question of his succession was supposedly raised at an assembly shortly before Duke Robert went on his pilgrimage to Jerusalem, one which would prove to be his last. Contemporary French monk William of Jumièges ("Jumièges" for short, to avoid confusion), the compiler of the magnificent *Gesta Normannorum Ducum* (*Deeds of the Norman Dukes*), stated that the nobles were dismayed when Robert announced his pilgrimage plans, giving the impression that it happened on the duke's whim. However, preparing for such a feat was not an easy affair. In fact, it would cost a lot of money, and it would take weeks, more often than not even months, to prepare. And considering that the distance between the ducal palace at Fécamp and the city of Jerusalem is close to 4,400 km (over 2,700 miles) and that the rulers had to make this pilgrimage on horseback and, at times, by boat, it's safe to say that the decision to visit the Holy Land was anything but rushed or sudden. More to the point, other rulers in Normandy had already been on pilgrimages to Jerusalem, with one of Robert's adversaries, Count Fulk Nerra of Anjou, visiting the city no less than four times before 1039 (two of those were during Robert's lifetime).

The assembly that Jumièges wrote of was most likely held at Fécamp, with some of the most prominent magnates being in attendance. Supposedly, King Henry I of France confirmed the arrangements of the assembly, possibly as one of the ways of repaying Robert's support during the king's aforementioned quarrel with his mother. During this assembly, Robert asked the lords to acknowledge William as his successor and to obey the young boy as their military commander and the rightful heir while he was on his trip to Jerusalem. The nobility readily accepted young William, and there were even extensive negotiations among the local princes to safeguard the realm and help the boy out while his father was away on his pilgrimage.

Robert's death eventually came; the duke passed away in Nicaea on July 2nd, 1035, on his way back from Jerusalem after contracting an illness.

A few decades later, people would claim that the duke was poisoned. However, there's no evidence to suggest any type of foul play. When the news of Robert's death reached Fécamp, William officially became the ruler of Normandy, despite being an eight-year-old boy. Interestingly, the dukes and princes all readily accepted the reign of the new young monarch, and there were no immediate attempts to end his life or dethrone him. As odd as it might sound, considering the frequent rate of both infanticide and political turmoil, the local nobles had very good reasons to maintain the status quo. After all, both Robert and his father Richard had an extensive network of connections across western Europe and were on good relations with Rome. Moreover, despite rebellions and uprisings being quite frequent among Norman dukes and princes, Robert and his ancestors managed to maintain some semblance of internal peace and stability. If the nobles were to remove young William or try to usurp him, they would lose vast territorial properties and more than likely end up dead. The same went for the high-ranking church officials in Normandy, who were quickly growing and expanding the influence of Norman Christianity by establishing connections with both France and southern Italy. More to the point, Robert had been known as a generous gift-giver to the Church, and these exploits were notable even during his trip to Jerusalem. Keeping William in power was a prudent move for both the clergy and the aristocracy.

Of course, we can't forget that William was a boy when his father died. The mere fact that Robert was embarking on a journey thousands of kilometers away, a journey that entailed far too many lethal perils, must have been stressful for the young heir apparent. It also must have been especially difficult for William because of how much he loved and respected both of his parents. The news of Robert dying in a foreign land must have, therefore, lay heavy on William's heart. It also didn't help that he was surrounded by members of the aristocracy, lots of whom he had barely met before in his life but who were going to be shaping him into a ruler for the years to come. And while the Norman princes did, in fact, stay loyal to the young duke and the legacy of his father, the psychological instability must have still been there. Adult William would prove himself to be quite a resilient figure who could endure (and commit) some of the worst atrocities, and it's not impossible to think that these traumatic events from his early childhood influenced his personality. However, that's merely speculation since dealing with trauma and anxiety at an early age can manifest quite differently during one's adult years.

One detail from his father's passing that definitely influenced William was the old duke's devotion to the Church and his extensive religious patronage. In his later years, William would seek to emulate this practice as often as possible.

William's Adolescence

William would officially act as a duke in 1042 when he was around fifteen years old. However, discerning his activities during the years of his minority, i.e., the years when he still required stewards to rule in his stead, is a difficult task.

Being a minority ruler (in other words, a monarch under the age where he or she can independently take power) was far from rare in medieval Europe, with some notable examples from the first few centuries of the 2nd millennium including Holy Roman Emperors Otto III and Henry IV and French King Philip I. The biggest problem with minority rulers was the almost inevitable potential for instability. On the one hand, children can be easily deposed, even if it doesn't involve outright murder. All it really takes is to rile up the crowds of either commoners or other nobles who would see a child as an unfit ruler, and the exchange would happen quickly. Moreover, during a crisis, a child ruler would not only prove to be ineffective (most child rulers are unable to provide sound strategic advice and proper fiscal policies during a civil war, rebellion, or outside invasion) but also a hindrance to his or her subjects.

But the deposition of minority rulers was not the only setback of this type of rule. Namely, guardians and stewards who would govern the land in the place of the young monarch could present a whole other host of problems. For instance, an influential regent, like John Hunyadi in Hungary in the 1400s, could become powerful enough to earn the sympathies of both the commoners and the nobles, and soon enough, he or she would claim power or at the very least secure power for their successors (which is what Hunyadi did for his son Matthias, who later became the king of Hungary). That kind of influence could bring an end to the ruling dynasty and cause political and social turmoil within the monarchy.

In William's time, at least two separate people are noted as being his guardians during his early adolescence. One of them was Count Gilbert of Brionne, whose father was the half-brother of William's grandfather, Duke Richard II. The other man was the son of Robert's sister Hawise, Count Alan III of Brittany. They, alongside Alan's brother Count Eudo, were all prominent figures in contemporary Normandy, with Alan, in particular, being busy protecting the south of Normandy from the forces of Anjou.

The names and familial relations of these men should not surprise anyone since nepotism was quite frequent in both the medieval courts and the Church. During William's minority, for instance, he had one powerful ally who effectively ruled Normandy while Robert was on his way to Jerusalem: Archbishop Robert II of Rouen. Robert II, who was both an archbishop of Rouen and a count of Évreux, was the son of Duke Richard I, making him Duke Robert's uncle and William's granduncle. The two

Roberts, the archbishop and the duke, were actually at odds with each other, with the duke banishing the old priest for a while and the priest excommunicating the youth in return. However, they would later be reconciled, and Duke Robert would attempt to atone for his transgressions by lavishly gifting churches and priests, which William had to have witnessed.

However, the fact that he was directly related to Richard I is key here, for his position as the archbishop of Rouen was succeeded by Malger (or Mauger), William's uncle. Archbishop Robert's son, Richard, took over as the count of Évreux sometime after 1037. In other words, nepotism was still in full effect by the time William assumed power, with most of the people in high places being either his close or distant cousins.

Interestingly, the fates of both Count Gilbert and Count Alan are linked to individuals who would play prominent roles in William's life. Gilbert, William's tutor, was known to be a bit self-aggrandizing and arrogant, which earned him enemies throughout his life. He was killed in Échauffour in 1040, and the assassins acted under the orders of Ralph de Gacé, the middle son of Archbishop Robert of Rouen. Later in life, this cousin of William's would help force Thurstan of Goz, a nobleman, out of Falaise, and soon enough, he would come to be a part of William's inner circle, being a leader of the young duke's army until his death in 1051.

Alan, on the other hand, died at Vimoutiers on October 1st, 1040, most likely falling ill during the siege of a nearby town, though some sources claim he fell ill at Vimoutiers and died while returning to Fécamp.

The context behind Alan's death was the ongoing conflict between William's guardians and Roger I of Montgomery. The conflict arose after the death of Archbishop Robert in 1037. Anarchy broke out, and Roger I led the rebellion against the established powers. Osbern the Steward, one of William's oldest tutors and advisors, forced Roger I into exile, taking his territories away from him. While Roger was at the court of King Henry I in Paris, his son, William, actually managed to enter the Norman palace and kill Osbern but was soon swiftly dispatched himself. This incident was, by far, the closest that William came to death as a child. However, the end of this rebellion did result in the young duke gaining two allies who would prove invaluable in his later exploits: William Fitz Osbern and Roger II of Montgomery. In other words, two of the most active members of Duke William's entourage were the sons of people who had on opposite sides of that rebellion.

Early Reign

With William now in power, there was a lot that needed to be done. The country had been in turmoil since the rebellion, and the young ruler clearly had to assert some sort of power over his realm. In around 1043, he won his first military campaign against Thurstan of Goz. Thurstan sought help from King Henry I of France, who had been supporting some of William's opponents, including Count Fulk Nerra of Anjou, who had died three years earlier. King Henry wanted to consolidate power in Normandy, which would explain his attempts at undermining William during his minority years. However, King Henry was the one who had legitimated the young duke's succession when Robert was preparing to go to Jerusalem, and the alliance between France and Normandy was technically still going strong. He would soon prove to be an important ally of William during his early reign.

William needed to directly engage in local warfare for a few reasons. The first and obvious one was the fact that he needed to show personal assertiveness and ambition to rule. But the other reason might have played a more key role; namely, Henry I was exhibiting the same type of "peace-keeping" power that Robert had, just as Richard II before him had.

William wanted and needed to make sure the people had a conciliator that was of the Norman ducal family.

William was proactive even in these early days. He would lead skirmishes against both the negative elements in his own dukedom as well as the people outside of its borders. In addition, he would actively appoint or dismiss people at the ducal court; this was definitely based on personal preferences but not without taking merit into account. A vast number of these were dukes and counts who were prominent during the era of both William's father and his grandfather, such as Archbishop Malger of Rouen, Ralph Taisson, and Godfrey, the Vicomte of Arques. And while there were both familial and professional ties between these men and the ducal family, they don't necessarily show William's preference of choosing whomever he pleased, which can be seen in his choice for other prominent members of his court. The first two have already been mentioned: William Fitz Osbern and Roger II of Montgomery, whose fathers were bitter enemies. The third was Roger of Beaumont, son of Humphrey de Vieilles and a member of the high aristocracy.

The Beaumonts were actually in the middle of a famed family feud with a different house, that of Tosny. Both families had extensive wealth and territories, which led to some disputes. In addition, both were among the first Norman aristocratic families to found their own Benedictine abbeys. The Tosnys were eventually crushed by Roger of Beaumont, but William's court had to act fast to stabilize the situation as efficiently as possible. All of the surviving members of the House of Tosny were married off to either major or minor nobility in Normandy, thus allowing William to both quash the feud between the two families and maintain some semblance of peace.

In addition to quashing feuds in order to maintain peace among his subjects, William was no stranger to strategic marriages outside of the borders of his dukedom. For instance, one of his foes at the time, Count William of Arques, married the sister of Count Enguerrand II of Ponthieu in an attempt to stabilize the eastern border of Normandy. Count Enguerrand married William's own sister, Adelaide, further solidifying the alliance between the duke and the count and strengthening upper Normandy. In addition to these marriages, William also gifted Arques with some land, which made the count effectively independent despite his alliance with the young duke. Of course, the two marriages and the landholdings would not prove to be a permanent solution, considering that both William of Arques and Enguerrand II were in open rebellion against Duke William in 1052. Nevertheless, it was still a proactive move on William's part in several respects. First off, it showed that he was willing to forgive past transgressions to his former foes by gifting land to them (he did the same with Thurstan of Goz, as his family was allowed to own land later during William's reign). Next, it showed that William was more concerned with maintaining order than showing off power, at least to an extent.

Gifting churches and transferring church relics were also a part of young William's repertoire, with one particular anecdote stating that he postponed the dedication of the church near Caen until he himself had brought the reliquary there on his shoulders. The combination of this practice with the strategic marriages, restoring the property of various monasteries, and maintaining order throughout the dukedom is a great indicator of things to come in the duke's later life; even as early as fifteen, William showed a proactive, positive stance on maintaining unity and peace among his subjects, a practice that would translate well into his kingly years.

Young William's minority, it seems, went well, rebellions and skirmishes notwithstanding. He made new friends, reigned in foes, maintained his father's old contacts, forged new ones, gifted churches, and appointed officials. However, by the late 1040s, the young duke would find himself at the forefront of multiple wars, which would test both his military prowess and his abilities as a ruler. Moreover, they were going to shape the things to come both in Normandy and beyond. William, with his new entourage, had been growing into quite a political force in the region, and it was only natural that the people around him, friends and foes alike, started to take notice.

Chapter 2 – The Conquest: Normandy and Britain in the Late 10th Century, the Battle of Hastings, and the Aftermath

Normandy in the Late 10th Century: Consolidating Power

The Battle of Val-ès-Dunes

The Battle of Val-ès-Dunes took place in 1047 when William was around nineteen years of age. While we don't know many details about the battle itself, it would prove to be the decisive factor in establishing William as the ruler of the Normans. The war was waged between the young duke and the coalition of rebel nobles, which was headed by Guy of Burgundy, the Count of Brionne.

Early historians assumed that the reason behind Guy's rebellion was due to William's supposed illegitimacy. As stated earlier, no noble during William's time considered William to be a bastard, hence illegitimate to inherit Robert's throne. However, it is true that Guy had the aim of taking the throne from William, considering he had familial ties to the royal family. He was William's first cousin (Guy's mother was Alice, Duke Richard II's sister), but more notably, he was the younger son of Count Reginald I, making him unable to ascend the throne. As a child, Guy was sent to the Norman court, where he was William's childhood companion for a short time. When his cousin, Gilbert of Brionne, died in 1040, Guy received his lands at Brionne and was also gifted the land of Vernon.

Guy clearly wanted to expand his influence and make a name for himself, so claiming the title of duke of Normandy was the most direct way to do it. As a child, and a younger son at that, he had no resources to achieve this feat, but it wouldn't have been hard for him to amass some support among the nobles who were dissatisfied with young William's reign. This list included some notable individuals:

- Ranulf of Bessin
- Haimo Dentatus ("Haimo the Toothy")
- Ralph Taisson, lord of Harcourt-Thury
- Nigel of Cotentin
- Grimoult du Plessis-Grimoult

Almost all of these nobles were aging and set in their ways, while William and most of his entourage (Fitz Osbern, Roger of Montgomery, and Roger of Beaumont) were young and ambitious men who were governing affairs in their own way. Of course, Nigel and Guy were roughly the same age as William, but as we've established, Guy had his own reasons for going after the throne, and Nigel, whose family had close ties with the rulers of Burgundy, probably helped out of a sense of duty or possibly even genuine amicable closeness with Guy's family.

Early accounts suggest that Guy's co-conspirator Grimoult tried to assassinate William at Valognes in either late 1046 or early 1047, and the young duke first fled to Ryes-en-Bessin and from there to Poissy, a town near Paris, to meet up with King Henry I. William was aware that Guy's allies were at Valognes, well into the Duchy of Normandy's territory. William's presence so close to the enemy might have been an effort to either calm the situation down or plan a preemptive strike of his own. Whatever the case might be, William's retreat was merely a temporary setback.

In the summer of 1047, the duke would come back to Normandy to rally his troops, suggesting that despite the rebels' strength, the current regime still had support. Who precisely supported William, aside from the French king, we don't know for certain. King Henry I's army would meet William's at Caen, and interestingly enough, one of the rebels actually defected to William's side. Despite having been a part of the rebellion, which had an advantage in numbers (supposedly, the rebels amassed an army of 25,000 men, while the combined forces of William and Henry I barely amounted to 10,000), Ralph Taisson decided to shift his allegiance and join William in his cause.

The two armies met at the plain of Val-ès-Dunes. Initially, the rebels had the advantage due to sheer numbers; however, their leadership was nowhere near as tight-knit as that of William and Henry. Contemporary authors, such as William of Poitiers (Duke William's chaplain and the author of *Gesta Willelmi ducis Normannorum et regis Anglorum*, or *The Deeds of William, Duke of the Normans and King of the English*) and Jumièges, place a decent amount of significance to the role King Henry played in the battle, though admittedly, Jumièges did that more so than

Poitiers. While it's not impossible that the majority of soldiers belonged to Henry and that he might have been the one in command, it's also likely that Jumièges simply wrote that down to acknowledge the king's high status and power, as monks usually did back in the day when writing about prominent rulers. Whatever the case might be, it doesn't lessen William's accomplishments in this battle.

As stated, we don't know the exact details of the battle, but from what we can ascertain, William's forces were losing in the beginning, but thanks to some tactical flanking on their part, the rebels soon broke apart and scattered. Supposedly, William's and Henry's armies drove them all the way to the river Orne, where the fleeing troops drowned en masse. No historian of the time mentions any prisoners being taken, which would mean that William and Henry slaughtered the survivors. This type of brutality wasn't common among the Norman dukes or any other ruler in western Europe at the time, but it would have helped William solidify his victory on the battlefield. The main conspirator, Guy, retreated to his well-fortified castle at Brionne, which William would besiege for more than two years until Guy submitted. Despite his actions, William pardoned Guy and allowed him to stay at his court, though this was likely done to keep him in check, a "house prison" of sorts. In addition to this humiliation, Guy also lost all of his castles and territories.

William's victory at Val-ès-Dunes was neither easy nor a surefire way of consolidating power. In fact, there were still people in his realm who openly wanted him gone. After the battle had concluded, these same nobles were forced to declare a so-called "Truce of God," by which they were prohibited from having small-scale wars on certain days of the week. Conversely, neither William nor Henry had to abide by this rule. In short, no noble was allowed to start wars during certain days, but if William felt like it, he could go after anyone at any time.

Despite the difficulty of William's military achievement, the campaign had been a success. With this action, William had shown his fellow Normans that he was every bit the duke his father and the fathers before him were and that he was more than capable of staving off an enemy twice his size. Moreover, even though William had suffered losses, and there was still a risk of a major rebellion, no new revolts would happen until five years later.

Commemorative column at the site of the Battle of Val-ès-Dunes
Roi.dagobert, CC BY-SA 3.0 <https://creativecommons.org/licenses/by-sa/3.0>, via Wikimedia Commons https://commons.wikimedia.org/wiki/File:Colonne_Vimont.jpg

The Siege of Brionne

When we take a look at the years that followed the Battle of Val-ès-Dunes, it might seem odd to learn that Duke William had spent several of them besieging Brionne, the castle where Guy of Burgundy shut himself in after losing the battle. Now, the length of the siege (three years, at most) is not the odd part since there are other well-known historical sieges that lasted more than twice as long as the one at Brionne. For example, in the famous Siege of Candia, where approximately 60,000 Ottoman Turks laid siege to the Venetian city in question, the Venetians held out for an astounding twenty-two years. What you might find odd, though, is that the siege was laid with William being absent for the majority of its duration. As early as May 23rd, 1048 (on Whitsun, also known as the Pentecost), which was roughly a year after his victorious battle, William would be present at King Henry's court in Senlis. One of the people present at this assembly was Baldwin V, Count of Flanders. The events that follow would prove to be crucial for William in the next few years.

In 1049, most likely as a result of the Whitsun assembly the year before, King Henry I would lead a campaign against Geoffrey Martel of Anjou, the son of the late Count Fulk Nerra. Martel had been an ally of Holy Roman Emperor Henry III, who had been waging a long war against Baldwin and his allies. Two important takeaways stem from these events. The first is that Baldwin would have three children, with one of them being a daughter named Matilda. Matilda would become the wife of William and the future queen of England. Most likely, the two men had discussed the potential marriage as early as 1048 in Senlis. But more importantly, the conflict between Flanders, France, and other western territories on the one hand, and the Holy Roman Empire and Anjou on the other, saw two more men join the fray: Earl Godwine of Essex and Edward the Confessor. Interestingly, they were effectively opponents in this conflict, with Edward assisting the Holy Roman emperor, while Godwine (also spelled as Godwin) would frequently use Flanders as a refuge in troubled times. We'll go into both Edward and Godwine in more detail a little later, but it's safe to say that William's eventual conquest of England didn't come out of anywhere and that his reasoning traces its roots to right here.

Nearly all of the events that would change William's life happened during the siege of Brionne. The reason behind its long duration is largely

William's confidence, perhaps even a hint of cheekiness. William knew very well that Guy had no remaining allies. Even people who would vouch for him, such as Nigel of Cotentin, continued to hold office as William's underlings, once again showing William's willingness to forgive past transgressions. And we should make no mistake—Brionne was a formidable fortress, one of the few of its kind in Normandy. Located on an island between two branches of the river Risle, it was nigh-impenetrable at the time, and a typical active siege would have exhausted William's resources. However, he purposefully persisted until the garrison at the fort was undergoing severe starvation, forcing Guy to surrender in 1049. Not only would William have constantly put pressure on the fort via his troops, but he also commissioned the construction of earthwork forts on both sides of the river, effectively cutting off all supply routes to the castle.

Upon Guy's surrender, William allowed him to stay at his court, in what was basically house arrest. However, unlike the other opponents at the Battle of Val-ès-Dunes, Guy chose to exile himself to his native Burgundy, where he would attempt to snag power from his older brother, William the Great (colloquially also known as William the Stubborn). Some of Guy's closest allies, like Nigel, would actually accompany Duke William during his 1066 campaign and even go so far as to make a name for themselves during combat. However, despite his merits on the battlefield, Nigel didn't receive any lands in England, showing, perhaps, that even William's propensity for forgiveness had its limits in terms of consequences.

As a young man of twenty, Duke William was already showing a vast array of personal qualities that make a great leader, at least according to Poitiers and other medieval authors of the time. His prudence and patience proved invaluable during the siege of Brionne, and his willingness to forgive and employ his former foes was once again on full display.

Moreover, he showed great skills in battle, such as strategic approaches to attacks, resilience in the face of danger, and the capability of taking calculated risks. But his genius was on display even outside of battle. Within his native Normandy, William began elevating his closest allies into positions of power within the Church. His own half-brother, Odo, became the bishop of Bayeux after the death of Bishop Hugh in the autumn of 1049. Hugh's land around the bishopric would come to belong to his nephew, William Fitz Osbern. And speaking of Fitz Osbern, we should mention another detail that directly relates to William's future exploits. William Fitz Osbern's brother, Osbern Fitz Osbern, crossed the English Channel at some point in 1050 in order to become a cleric, and soon enough, he was the chaplain to none other than King Edward the Confessor.

The late 1040s and early 1050s would prove to be the most difficult years of William's tenure as the duke of Normandy. The south of his land was under constant threat by Anjou, which intensified when a certain Ivo, Bishop of Sées, succeeded to the lordship of the Bellême. It was made even more serious when Geoffrey Martel invaded and occupied Maine in 1051. Martel was one of the most powerful lords in the region at that time, and William's decision to go to war with him showed not only a huge level of confidence but also brazen bravery.

William's Foes: The Hardest Period

Tensions were high between Normandy and Anjou, and it didn't help that William's marriage to Matilda was banned by Pope Leo IX at the Council of Rheims in the autumn of 1049. The reason behind the ban was the fact that Matilda and William shared the same ancestor, the Scandinavian Viking ruler Rollo, who had managed to secure lands for his Norsemen among the Franks. In fact, the whole region of Normandy specifically has that name because of the influx of Scandinavians in the early 10th century.

That brings us to an interesting aside in regards to the Normans. While they spoke French and were integrated with the Francophone culture of the region, Normans are actually descendants of Germanic Scandinavian warriors. So, technically, the Norman invasion of England wasn't done by the French but by French-speaking Germans who, in all likelihood, share some common ancestry with the Anglo-Saxons who were inhabiting England at the time.

However, in terms of war, things were about to get much more complicated for William. His successes and newfound reputation didn't sit well with one of his most powerful allies, King Henry I of France. As stated earlier, Henry, much like William, wanted to be the most influential political factor in the region and to expand French influence over as many territories as possible. The timing was quite convenient, considering that there were nobles who were openly against the duke's regime and who would have happily seen someone else take the ducal throne. It wouldn't be an exaggeration to claim that the war between William, on the one hand, and Martel and Henry, on the other, would have been the single most important battle for the region, as well as a clash between two of the most formidable forces in western Europe at the time.

The first sparks of war came soon after Martel took Maine in 1051. As early as the following year, William laid siege to two important towns: Alençon and Domfront. Alençon, in particular, was important to William since it had been a Norman-held territory for generations; in his eyes, he had to reclaim it. With that in mind, the duke first laid siege to Domfront, which saw Geoffrey Martel withdraw, but the town still held out on its own and refused to surrender. Without taking the town, William's forces moved to Alençon, and the town surrendered quickly after a particular incident. Namely, the garrison was beating the skins to draw William's attention and mocking his heritage, or rather, specifically mocking the heritage of his mother, Herleva. Reportedly, William was so beside himself with rage that he ordered his soldiers to storm the town, burn it, and mutilate the mockers by having their hands and feet lopped off. With the quick surrender of Alençon, William moved back to Domfront, which surrendered upon hearing the news from the other town.

But William had no time to rest. Aside from the trouble brewing from the Angevin side, he had to deal with another, older threat, that of his uncle William of Arques. Despite receiving lands from his nephew, Arques had apparently denounced his oath of vassalage and started plotting his own rebellion against William. In terms of support, not many local lords were on Arques's side, but he did have one notable ally within the duchy—William's other uncle, Archbishop Malger. The two men, evidently led by greed and the desire to expand their influence, worked hard on deposing William as early as 1049 when Arques supposedly abandoned the duke in the middle of the Battle of Val-ès-Dunes (though there are no records that confirm this treachery, it's not improbable that it might have happened considering the history between William and his uncle). Arques also managed to secure an alliance with King Henry and Geoffrey Martel, and he still had the support of Enguerrand II, the Count of Ponthieu, who had once been married to William's sister Adelaide. Now leading a full-on revolt, Count William of Arques started to raid the countryside surrounding Arques as a means of intimidating the young duke.

Duke William would besiege Arques in a similar way as Brionne. He would build siege forts in strategic locations around the town and leave his men to handle the siege itself while he was off doing other important business. The rebellion of Count William lasted from 1052 to roughly 1054, the very height of activity on the part of Geoffrey Martel and King

Henry. On October 25th, 1053, William's troops that were stationed at the siege castle ambushed a relieving force sent by King Henry at Saint-Aubin-sur-Seine, during which Count Enguerrand was killed. William himself recounted this event on his deathbed, claiming that his troops took care of the situation before he had managed to arrive and calling the count a valiant knight. Despite Enguerrand not being his sister's husband anymore, and despite being on the opposing side, William still spoke of the count with high praise years later.

William would eventually defeat this French force and go back to besieging Arques. Once the troops inside were starved and could no longer take it, Guy surrendered to his nephew in 1054. Historical accounts aren't in agreement when it comes to the aftermath, but the most likely course of events had William exile Guy, who then fled to Boulogne to the court of Count Eustace II, another ruler who would be a prominent name in the Battle of Hastings twelve years later. Despite exiling him, and despite Guy's history of rebellious behavior, William sent him off with lavish monetary gifts. Arques would be the last of his line to be the count of his land, and his later years and death remain unknown to us.

Battle of Mortemer

The year 1054 would see the first major victory against the coalition of King Henry I and Geoffrey Martel, and it would show just how tightly knit the Norman princes acted when defending William's throne and how disjointed the French-Angevin alliance really was. The king's forces were led by his brother Odo, and after assembling in northeastern France, they soon joined up with troops commanded by Count Renaud of Claremont and, more importantly, Count Guy of Ponthieu, the brother of the recently deceased Enguerrand. Other prominent opponents of William were Count Theobald II of Blois and Duke William VII of Aquitaine, though they weren't necessarily willing to fight for the French king and might have only answered the summons in order to reduce William's power for their own gain.

The invading forces started to devastate eastern Normandy, launching a two-pronged attack. One faction took hold of the castle Evrecin, which initially seemed like a victory. However, the faction that went after Mortemer was met with an unpleasant surprise. The united forces of Count Robert of Eu (one of William's most powerful supporters), Lord Walter Giffard of Longueville, Roger, Hugh de Gournay, and William of Warenne crushed the invading force in an incredibly difficult battle that saw Guy of Burgundy captured and the invaders scatter. Roger would come to be known as Roger I of Mortemer after gaining possession of the castle, but he would be banished from it not long after due to providing shelter to one of William's enemies. William of Warenne, Roger's supposed cousin, would come to own the castle, but Roger kept the name "Mortemer," making him the first Norman in history with that name.

The victory at Mortemer ended with a truce between William and Henry, and one of the conditions of this truce was that William got to keep all of the Angevin territories he had taken during the battle. He was even allowed to invade farther into Anjou if he so wished. However, this condition wasn't officially a part of the peace agreement, so future conflicts were inevitable. William's victory over the allied forces under King Henry had proven one thing without a shadow of a doubt—the young duke was becoming a powerful man, and the entire paradigm of regional power was slowly being rewritten.

After the victory, William had one more loose end to tie up. His uncle, Archbishop Malger, was implicated to have been conspiring with William of Arques; thus, he had to be removed. Sometime in 1055, a synod was held in Lisieux, an important center of power for the medieval Normans and a center of a prominent bishopric. William evidently followed protocol to the letter and had Malger removed legally, replacing him with a Rheims-born bishop called Maurilius. This particular choice for the new archbishop is quite important, considering that Maurilius was not related to William in any way. The practice at the time, as we have seen earlier, was to appoint close family members in order to earn favors with the Church and to prevent future dynastic disputes. Since William was becoming more open and welcoming of advice from Norman Church officials (such as Lanfranc of Bec, a famous Italian bishop who would become the archbishop of Canterbury and an important part of William's rule in England), he chose Maurilius specifically because of his prowess as a bishop and his apparent moral and spiritual qualities.

Malger was banished from Rouen to the isle of Guernsey in the English Channel. Wace, a Norman poet who lived a century after these events took place, collected stories about Malger's final years on the island. Apparently, at least according to these stories, the deposed archbishop married and fathered numerous children, had a pet goblin named *Toret* ("little Thor"), engaged in hawking and reading the occult, made a pact with the devil, and eventually drowned in 1055. Of course, most of these stories are contradictory; for instance, he would have been unable to have numerous children with the same wife, as he was deposed in early 1055 and had, presumably, died the same year. But the mere presence of these stories at least hints that he was still a well-known priest and political figure in the region. His remains are supposedly in a church somewhere in the Cotentin Peninsula.

Duke William of Normandy sending a herald to King Henry 1, 14th century, British Library
https://commons.wikimedia.org/wiki/File:William%2BHenry_2.jpg

Battle of Varaville

It would be three years until both King Henry and Geoffrey Martel invaded Normandy again. By that time, the ban on William's marriage was likely lifted; in fact, it was possible that it might have been lifted as early as 1050. Matilda bore him at least two sons before the Battle of Varaville: the eldest Robert and the younger Richard (they were born in around 1053/54 and 1055, respectively). William Rufus, the future king of England, was born c. 1060. Of his daughters, Adeliza and Cecilia were surely born in the 1050s, while Constance and Matilda were born sometime before the campaign of 1066. It was during this time that Herleva passed away; she was supposedly buried at Grestain Abbey. William held this abbey in high regard, as it was founded by his mother and his stepfather, Herluin, who would remain prominent until his death a little before 1066.

The fact that William had at least two (and, at most, four) healthy children before 1057 proves that both William and Matilda were in peak physical condition, considering that the mortality rate of children in early medieval times was incredibly high and that very few children lived to see adulthood. William's strong marriage and growing family also proves that his relationship with Rome had become more stable over time and that, at least in some matters, he was getting papal support. All of these indicators showed that William's status within his homeland was more secure than ever before, causing his power and influence to grow. Fewer and fewer lords had the courage to openly rebel against the duke, fearing swift retaliation from him and his many allies.

William negotiated peace with his opponents for years after the Battle of Mortemer, and one of the reasons it took so long was the duke's treatment of his prisoners. By far, his most valuable prisoner was Guy of Ponthieu, whom he held captive at Bayeux for at least two years. Upon release, Guy was to do homage to William, pay him perpetual fealty, and provide a hundred warriors to the duke every year. It's also suggested that he had to give up lands in Aumale, which were now governed by Adelaide, William's sister. This sort of treatment would have secured Guy's fealty in the short term, but he was far from enthusiastic about supporting his former foe, and the length of William's negotiations for prisoner releases didn't go over well with King Henry and Geoffrey Martel. And while a future conflict was far from unexpected, this treatment of Guy and other prisoners wasn't the only impetus for the duke's old foes to attack him again in 1057. Namely, William had constructed a castle just south of Domfront and north of Mayenne, near the town of Ambrières. Baron Geoffrey was the ruler of Mayenne, and William saw him as the biggest threat on the border. Understandably concerned, Geoffrey summoned Martel, who came along with several other nobles and besieged the new castle. However, the very second Martel caught wind of William marching to defend his territory, Martel and his forces fled, leaving Geoffrey by himself. Geoffrey had to swear fealty to William then and there, and his life was ultimately spared, but he would prove to be one of William's most enduring enemies throughout the duke's lifetime. After William's victory, the duke had a close supporter of the rebels, Vicomte Nigel, exiled, and the churches on

Guernsey, which belonged to Nigel, were granted to Marmoutier Abbey. In addition, Nigel's half-sister Muriel was married to a certain Eudo, the son of Thurstan Haldup, who was the founder of Lessay Abbey. Eudo was a rival to Cotentin and was, by extension, an enemy of Nigel's.

During this time, William was present at the consecration of the church at Coutances, where the new bishop, Geoffrey of Montbray, would start his lengthy and controversial career (from his very first days in "office," he was accused of simony, i.e., buying his position). Geoffrey would be an important figure in both the Battle of Hastings and the subsequent events in England.

All of these events took place before 1057, the year of the last foreign invasion of Normandy during William's lifetime. King Henry and Geoffrey Martel started to march, with their ultimate goal being Caen and Bayeux. They first arrived at Hiémois, where they did their fair share of looting and plundering to flush William out. William, however, merely gathered his troops and waited, sending the occasional scout from time to time to monitor the situation. The invading troops arrived at the estuary of the Dives river, which was near Varaville, but the lands they tried to cross were marshy and incredibly difficult to traverse.

Prudently waiting for them to cross, William surprised them with a rear attack, scattering the opposing army almost immediately. Both Henry and Martel fled the battle, barely surviving. But their armies that remained suffered more than just a crushing defeat. William ordered nearly every single soldier to be killed on the spot, and the massacre that took place was harsh enough to be written about by even his most ardent supporters. While William had committed atrocities before (such as his order of mutilation at Alençon), this example of violence was on a whole new level, even beyond the contemporary norms of Normandy or medieval western Europe in general. The few prisoners William did take, he scattered all across Normandy, which was far from the homeland of any of these prisoners.

While, historically speaking, the Battle of Varaville is important, as it was a turning point for both William and his foes, if we're speaking in the context of the warring sides themselves, as well as the authors who wrote of it at the time, it was of little consequence or relevance. First of all, the army of the rebels was nowhere near as powerful nor as numerous as it had been in 1053, for example. Of course, we don't have any real numbers of the troops on either side, but all we have to do is look at the number of supporters for each cause. Aside from Henry, Martel, and Geoffrey of Mayenne, there were barely any powerful or even mediocre allies who wanted to back the French and the Angevines. In fact, considering how patiently and prudently William had approached the war, as well as his protracted peace negotiations and prisoner releases, it's safe to say that the duke was well aware of his enemies' military impotence. Second of all, the power of William was such that nearly everyone at the time was on his side, whether they liked it or not. The Catholic Church saw no real issue with his rule, his marriage to Matilda had borne fruit, his close companions were receiving land and privileges that would secure their lot in life, and even his enemies would, more often than not, avoid incurring his wrath after a rebellion or a betrayal. Even when they did face punishment, it would usually come with a pardon a year or so later, with some added bonuses in terms of territory and gifts. But most importantly, Normandy was feeling like a united land, and it would sow the seeds for what William's cross-Channel "empire" would look like. And yes, the word "empire" here is appropriate even as early as 1066, one can see the early beginnings of what the proper British Empire would look like. Both the modern English Commonwealth and the earlier forms of the empire (the Raj in India, the East India Company, the colonies in Africa, etc.) would effectively be the same as William's kingdom-to-come. William had gone from an upstart young man to a full-fledged ruler in a period of fourteen years, amassing a legion of followers and beating some of the most powerful regional lords. But his ambitions were far from quenched. There other areas around Normandy that were up for grabs, and soon enough, William would try an important, daring campaign that would go down in history.

England in the 1050s and the 1060s

Before moving into the years preceding the famed 1066 campaign, we should take a look at the events that were occurring in England. People who tend to have a limited knowledge of history often think that the reasons behind William's conquest were rather simple. Some would argue that he wanted to prove a point to the nobles of Normandy; apparently, being called a bastard wasn't something he was appreciative of, and he wanted to let the other nobles know what he was capable of (and, after all, being called "the Conqueror" sounds better than "the Bastard"). Others would argue that he simply used a politically expedient moment to move in and claim a kingdom that wasn't his to claim. However, the actual history behind William's initial plans of taking over England and the events that led to it are incredibly complex. They are almost a textbook example of medieval politics, and it is surprising how eerily similar it is to modern-day political intrigue.

During the reigns of William's immediate ancestors, as well as during his minority, England went through a lot. The House of Wessex was in power at the beginning of the century, with Æthelred II the Unready ruling as king until 1016. During his reign, he was briefly exiled to Normandy to live with his wife Emma's family. Emma was the daughter of Duke Richard I the Fearless and the aunt of the still unborn Duke William. This exile was the result of the advances of the Danish king, Sweyn Forkbeard. Danes claiming the throne of England wasn't exactly a new occurrence. In fact, plenty of Danish men and women had found a home in England since the 9th century, and kings like Sweyn would frequently attempt to take the throne away from the native Anglo-Saxon rulers.

Sweyn was a powerful ruler and a spectacular military strategist, but he didn't snatch the throne in the end. In February 1014, he died suddenly, which Æthelred used as a chance to return from his exile and retake the throne. He further humiliated the Danes by exiling Sweyn's son, Cnut.

While there was no real succession crisis in terms of Anglo-Saxon ruling houses (Æthelred had no less than eight sons, after all), the Wessex king had other problems. Namely, he was extremely unpopular among the people and the upper classes, and the nobles that he had wronged had essentially forced him to declare his loyalty to them, forgive all past transgressions, and issue a series of reforms that would benefit those very nobles greatly. Of course, Cnut wasn't taking his exile lying down. As the new king of Denmark, he retaliated against Æthelred, with his only real support within England coming from the lesser, former Kingdom of Lindsey, in modern North Lincolnshire. Æthelred allied himself with King Olaf II Haraldsson of Norway, who captured London using a powerful fleet and drove Cnut's men out. Both Olaf and Æthelred successfully managed to take London, and Cnut retreated from England completely, effectively leaving the people of Lindsey at Æthelred's mercy. For a while, Æthelred once again ruled a somewhat united England, apart from the Danelaw, i.e., the section of England heavily inhabited by descendants of the Danish Vikings from a century and a half ago.

Æthelred's good fortunes would come to an end as early as 1016. His son, Edmund, later to be known as King Edmund Ironside, broke off all ties and defected to the Danish. The reasons behind his defection lie in his marriage of Ealdgyth, the widow of Sigeferth, a thegn who had been on the side of Sweyn and Cnut and who had been killed by one of Æthelred's men, Eadric Streona. Ealdgyth was supposed to be brought to Malmesbury Abbey after the death of her husband, but Edmund took her as his wife, presumably to strengthen his own position in the East Midlands. Whatever the case may be, Edmund was now openly opposing his father.

Surprisingly, the Danelaw began to support Edmund in lieu of both Æthelred and Cnut, despite Cnut being their kinsman. It had barely been two years since Cnut had left the men of Lindsey and ran off from Æthelred's army, so his Danish blood and crown would mean little to the natives. On the other hand, Æthelred was less than merciful toward the people who had been abandoned, but he hadn't been a popular king to begin with. Edmund was probably the only chance the Danelaw had of a somewhat effective ruler, one who wouldn't massacre or abandon his subjects. In short, despite noble families and primogeniture playing a vital role within medieval society, in reality, the only real indicator of a good ruler to both high-born and common folk alike was that he (or she) treated their subjects well.

Cnut had a successful string of victories against the English after 1015. In the meantime, Edmund had rejoined his father since King Æthelred was no longer appearing on the battlefield, possibly due to illness, which was affecting the course of the war. Edmund raised an army, joining forces with lords such as Earl Uhtred of Northumbria. However, other lords, such as Streona, were bending the knee to Cnut, and after the occupation of Northumbria, Uhtred did the same and met a violent end. The Anglo-Saxons were slowly losing their ground, and the Danish were chipping off more and more of their land.

Æthelred died on April 23rd, 1016, and the councilors in London crowned Edmund as their new king. However, most of the Witan (the

Anglo-Saxon assembly of prominent elders) outside of London had already declared Cnut as the rightful ruler of the English. The battle between the two men was inevitable, and despite the nobility, in general, being on Cnut's side, Edmund managed to rally troops who were willing to die for him. The two kings faced off at the famed Battle of Assandun, whose location still remains a hotly-debated subject among scholars. Cnut won a decisive victory, with Edmund and his forces fleeing. A short while later, the two men would meet, and Edmund was forced into a treaty that greatly benefited Cnut but still managed to preserve at least an ounce of the Anglo-Saxon monarch's dignity. According to this treaty, Cnut took control of most of England, including Mercia and Northumbria, while Edmund remained the king of Wessex. In addition, whoever was to die first would inherit the English throne.

This inheritance would come to pass sooner than expected. Edmund Ironside died on November 30th of that same year. Most contemporary sources claim that he had been murdered in some way, either by knife or crossbow, while he was relieving himself in the privy. However, the more likely answer is that he had simply succumbed to his wounds. The past few years before his death, which was essentially his entire reign, was a constant string of one war after another. With his death, Wessex became annexed by Cnut, who was now legally the sole ruler of a united England.

In many ways, Edmund was similar to William, taking a proactive role during a crisis and being able to rally many loyal troops in a heartbeat, despite the overwhelming odds. His contemporaries, even beyond Lindsey, must have seen him as a determined king who knew how to inspire loyalty and bravery in others. In fact, Cnut himself visited Edmund's tomb and placed a cloak decorated with depictions of peacocks onto it as a means of assisting Edmund's salvation. The peacock was a symbol of resurrection at the time. It's stunning to learn that even in one of the bloodiest periods of English history, bitter opponents would still find a way to respect one another. Edmund's reign might have been short and troubled (it barely lasted seven months), but even today, he is seen as one of the most respected English kings.

With Cnut now in power, events slowly began to unfold that would pave the way for William's eventual conquest of England. The new king had taken Emma of Normandy as his wife. Emma was Æthelred's widow and had borne him three children: Edward, Ælfred Ætheling (hereafter known as Alfred the Noble), and Godgifu of England (Goda in further text). Both of Emma's sons were sent to Normandy under the tutelage of her brother and William's grandfather, Duke Richard II. In the meantime, she would give birth to two of Cnut's children, a son named Harthacnut and a daughter named Gunhilda, the future wife of Holy Roman Emperor Henry III (the very same emperor who was an ally of Geoffrey Martel during some of William's hardest pre-Conquest years).

However, Cnut's marriage to Emma was far from regular. In fact, while she was his second wife, he had not annulled his marriage with Ælfgifu of Northampton, an important noblewoman from Mercia and the mother of Cnut's other two sons, Sweyn Knutsson and Harold Harefoot. Both men would rise to power, with Sweyn becoming the king of Norway and Harold the king of England for a brief period, but the very fact that Cnut had two simultaneous wives and male children with both made conflict inevitable, and the conflicts that would arise would affect no less than three different kingdoms (England, Norway, and Denmark).

It's instructive to pause for a moment and take a look at the broader picture in England. The kings of England had a direct connection, first by marriage and then by blood, with Normandy through Emma and her children. However, so did the Danish, and the offspring of this union would come to intermarry with some of the Normans' most prominent foes. Moreover, the English king had a potential conflict on his hands, as his sons by different wives could war with each other not only for the throne of England but also for the thrones of Denmark and Norway. And as we have seen, one of the sons of the former king of England was fighting on the side of the Normans' rivals, despite being directly related to them. It would be a massive understatement to claim that the situation was complicated beyond belief.

And if we take into account that William only needed to claim his familial connection to Emma in order to invade England, despite her only being his grandaunt, that opens a whole host of other possibilities. If he wanted, Cnut's son Harthacnut could have claimed the throne of Normandy in the same way, as could Edward the Confessor, simply on the basis of Richard II being their uncle. In a similar way, had Cnut's daughter borne Henry III male heirs, they could technically lay claim to the thrones of England, Normandy, or Denmark, despite being German emperors by way of their father's lineage. This labyrinthine network of familial ties is difficult enough without other elements, such as the Church, the other nobles, and the common folk, who all had an opinion on who should rule. For example, high church officials could easily oust a king or an emperor simply on the basis of this individual not acting like a proper Christian. In fact, Richard II exercised great effort into legitimizing his family in the eyes of the Church, considering how relatively new Normans were to Christianity at the time. In addition, he issued grants for various cathedrals, abbeys, monasteries, and other church-related buildings throughout his life, a practice that his successors (William very much included) would readily continue.

In terms of the nobles, we need only take a look at what was happening in Normandy from William's birth in around 1028 to his final victory over King Henry I and Count Geoffrey Martel in 1057. In less than three decades, the Normans saw a plethora of wars, rebellions, excommunications and restorations, exiles and returns, and punishments and pardons, both on the ecclesiastical and the political level. We see some dukes, counts, barons, vicomtes, and other nobles shifting their allegiance multiple times throughout their lives depending on convenience, without so much as taking William's lineage into account. And as fragmented as Normandy was, it was nothing compared to contemporary England at the time. It had barely been decades since the House of Wessex effectively united the island, or rather the part of the island roughly corresponding to modern-day England within the United Kingdom. And it didn't even take a few decades past that to see the Danes and the Anglo-Saxons fracture the country again to, yet again, reunite it under a non-English ruler. And last, but definitely not least, was the practice in which two rulers would reach an agreement of succession in the event of lacking any heirs or premature death. This practice was not that uncommon. In fact, it stems all the way back to the Roman period, and it was perfectly legal well after the fall of Constantinople in 1453, more than four centuries after William's birth. However, as is always the case, such deals are almost never put into practice without someone contesting them, such as a descendant of the former ruler, a distant relative, a relative of the new claimant, or even a complete outsider willing to take the throne by brute force.

All of the above is important in understanding just how complicated William's rise to the throne of England was and what it entailed. The two key men from England that would heavily influence this were Godwine (or Godwin), the Earl of Wessex, and Edward the Confessor, the future king of England and the son of Æthelred the Unready. Both men would spend a significant amount of time across the Channel, either in direct or indirect contact with the ruling families of Normandy and the surrounding countries while also meddling in local politics. Therefore, it is instructive to delve into both of these individuals to see how they relate to William and his future cross-Channel plans.

Earl Godwine of Wessex

Godwine's exact date of birth isn't known, nor his exact place of origin. However, we can ascertain that, while he was the earl of Wessex for most of his adult life, he was actually born somewhere in Sussex to a father of minor nobility. During the reign of Æthelred the Unready, Godwine was an adherent to the king's oldest son and heir apparent, Æthelstan. Upon his death in 1014, Æthelstan left Godwine a sizable piece of land in Compton, Sussex, which used to belong to Godwine's father, Wulfnoth Cild. A mere two years later, both Æthelred and his son Edmund would die, while the surviving issue of Æthelred would be either be exiled, outlawed, and then murdered, in that order (as was the case with his only surviving son from his first marriage, Eadwig Ætheling, in 1017), or simply exiled, as was the case with his children from his marriage with Emma of Normandy.

It was under Cnut that Godwine's rapid rise to prominence occurred. By 1020, eight years before William's birth, Godwine had been given the title of earl over all of Wessex, effectively making him the most powerful earl in the kingdom. In the following few years, he would accompany Cnut to Denmark, where the new king of England would assert his claim over the throne of the Danes following the death of their former king, Harald II. During this time, Cnut had to deal with the opposition of some Danes, as well as the Wends, a homogenous group of people (mainly Slavs) who were inhabiting Pomerania at the time. After Godwine led a supposed successful night raid against a Wendish encampment, he earned even more favor with Cnut. These good relations resulted in Godwine's marriage to Gytha Thorkelsdóttir. Gytha was a Danish noblewoman whose brother was Earl Ulf Thorgilsson. Ulf, in particular, is important because his descendants would rule Denmark for nearly 300 years. However, his marriage to Ulf's sister was important to Godwine because Ulf himself was married to Estrid Svendsdatter, Cnut's half-sister. In terms of politically expedient marriages, Godwine had struck gold; not only did he own a massive chunk of land in England, but he had also become even more closely linked to the king of England and Denmark with this marriage, making his station as secure as possible. The children that came from this marriage would play a prominent role in the events leading up to and including the Battle of Hastings, and one of Godwine's sons would be the last truly Anglo-Saxon king of England before William's conquest.

Godwine's career was stable in 1035 when Cnut died and his kingdom fractured. In Norway, Magnus the Good took power and ruled over both Norway and Denmark until 1047 (though he didn't ascend to the Danish throne until 1042). Magnus was the illegitimate son of King Olaf II, Cnut's predecessor in Norway, who was dethroned in 1030 after losing the famed Battle of Stiklestad due to some of his own men deserting him and switching sides. In England, Harold Harefoot, the son of Cnut and Ælfgifu, ruled as regent while Harthacnut, his half-brother, was busy consolidating power in Denmark. Harold hadn't officially been crowned king until 1037, presumably because the archbishop of Canterbury at the time, Æthelnoth, refused to crown him. A story from that time, which can't be verified by modern scholars, states that Æthelnoth only favored the sons Cnut had with his second wife, Emma, which was why he supposedly refused to crown Harefoot. Nevertheless, by 1037, Harold was officially the king, and during this year, the surviving children of Æthelred, Alfred the Noble and Edward the Confessor, returned to England from Normandy to lay claim to the throne. Historical accounts differ on this matter, but Earl Godwine was, in some way, responsible for the blinding and subsequent death of Alfred at Ely. Godwine also supposedly ordered that Alfred's retainers be severely dispatched, either through blinding, maiming, or scalping. Contemporary authors condemned these actions severely, and Edward would not forget these atrocities.

Harthacnut would succeed his half-brother Harold after the king's death in 1040. Apparently, the young king of Denmark, and now England, had been horrified when he heard what was done to his half-brother Alfred, an act Godwine was directly responsible for. Upon his arrival, Harthacnut ordered his men to exhume Harold's body, behead it, throw it into a fen, and finally fling it into the Thames, where it was later pulled out by fishermen and, unbeknownst to Harthacnut, buried by the Danes with proper honors. Despite his actions, Godwine did not lose his lands in Wessex and continued to act as an advisor to the new king. Harthacnut offered a full pardon to Godwine if he could prove that he was acting under direct orders from Harold. But instead of bringing witnesses, Godwine presented the king with a decorated ship that was valuable enough to pay for Godwine's eventual *wergild*. For clarification, in medieval Anglo-Saxon England, a wergild was the so-called "man price," i.e., the amount of money a noble had to pay to gain forgiveness for his past transgressions and effectively buy his own life. Even during these turbulent times, Godwine was one of the wealthiest men in England, if not outright the richest, and his position as earl remained as one of the most stable ones.

Harthacnut died under mysterious circumstances in 1042, though most historians believe that his death was the result of a stroke. For the first time in decades, the Danish reign over the English had ceased, as an Anglo-Saxon ruler was put on the throne. Godwine favored Edward the Confessor as the next king, though his rule would prove to be an unfavorable one for the earl. In order to understand the events that happened between 1042 and 1066 better, as well as the connection Godwine and his offspring have with it, let's shift our focus onto Edward and his life during the thirty years he spent in exile.

Return of Godwine and his sons to the court of King Edward the Confessor, 13ᵗʰ Century
https://commons.wikimedia.org/wiki/File:Return_of_Godwine.jpg

King Edward the Confessor

Edward is regarded as the last Anglo-Saxon king of a united England, or rather the last king of the House of Wessex to hold office, though neither of those statements is technically accurate. Edgar Ætheling, the grandson of Edmund Ironside and thus a grandnephew of Edward the Confessor, was technically chosen as the successor in 1066 by the Witan, but he was never officially crowned king, and his "reign" only lasted for several weeks at most. Nevertheless, he would technically be the last king of the House of Wessex, right after Edward. In addition, Edward's immediate successor, Harold Godwinson, was also partly Anglo-Saxon on his father's side, making him the last officially crowned Anglo-Saxon king; however, he was of mixed origin, considering his mother was a member of the Danish nobility. Of course, Edward was undisputedly the last Anglo-Saxon king to stay in office for a notable amount of time, namely twenty-four years (from 1042 to 1066).

Edward's early childhood, as well as the majority of his years spent outside of England, are not well known to history. According to contemporary sources, he would travel between mainland Europe and

England at least twice as a child. The first time was during his original exile during the Danish invasion under Sweyn in 1013. After Sweyn's death, Æthelred the Unready went back to England to claim the throne and sabotage Cnut from doing the same, and it was likely that Edward came with him. Folk tradition claims that after Æthelred's death, Edward took up arms alongside Edmund Ironside against Cnut, but considering that Edward would have been a thirteen-year-old boy at the time, this was highly unlikely. Upon Edmund's death, Edward once again went into exile in western Europe, with Normandy being the most probable location considering his family connections there. Cnut would end up marrying Edward's mother and killing his older half-brother Eadwig, effectively leaving Edward as the next in line from the House of Wessex to claim the English throne, should the opportunity arise.

Sometime in the early 1030s, Edward was in Normandy, signing a few charters in which he styled himself as "King of England." During this period, certain Norman church officials would openly declare their support of Edward as the king of England. However, his prospects of coming back to take the throne were slim at best. Most of the support he would have enjoyed in England was small or, more likely, silent during Cnut's reign. In addition, his mother, Emma, who was ambitious in her own way, favored her son Harthacnut as the successor, which he would eventually become after having consolidated power in Denmark. While he was among the Danes, Harold Harefoot acted as regent, and during his regency and subsequent kingship, Edward, alongside his brother Alfred, returned to England. As stated earlier, Alfred met a grisly end at the hands of Earl Godwine's men, which understandably angered both Edward and Harthacnut, as all three men shared the same mother. Edward himself had earned some positive reputation among the Normans and the Scandinavians for his military prowess, demonstrating it during a skirmish at Southampton, but he nevertheless retreated back to Normandy soon after.

Harthacnut invited Edward back to England, possibly at the urging of both Godwine and Ælfwine of Winchester, a bishop who gained prominence during Cnut's reign. The Danish king wanted to formally name Edward as his heir to the throne since he was unmarried and had no issue. It's tempting to think that Harthacnut did this out of familial love for his half-brother, considering that they had both lost Alfred several years prior. However, the succession was most likely an act of political expediency. Edward was the successor of the Wessex line and a direct descendant of Emma, who technically still held some form of power over Wessex itself. Moreover, Edward was getting support from the local nobles in England and Normandy, despite having lived most of his life in exile. Nevertheless, in 1041, Edward was back in England and was officially recognized as the successor.

There are some discrepancies over Edward's time in England both before and just after the coronation. He claimed that everyone in England accepted him as the new king, but this was highly unlikely or exaggerated. In reality, Edward would have been offered the throne only if he had agreed to continue to uphold Cnut's laws and maintain peace between the Anglo-Saxons and the Danes within the kingdom. In addition, he had to earn favor with three of the most powerful earls in the land, which wasn't easy since only one of them, Leofric of Mercia (the husband of the famous Lady Godiva), was the direct descendant of a family that had supported Edward's father during his reign. The Wessex line had been undermined by decades of Danish rule, and it showed even in the ruling makeup of English nobility at the time. Of the two remaining earls that had the biggest influence in England, Siward of Northumbria was, as his name suggests, anything but a native Northumbrian. He was Scandinavian, and some sources suggest he might have been a relative of Ulf, which would make sense since Cnut had the habit of bestowing English earldoms to the Danish. The final earl whose power Edward had to rein in was none other than Godwine, the same man who had his brother killed. Despite the evident animosity between these two men, they both had to move forward in order to maintain the kingdom. Godwine was one of the men who actually pursued Edward's ascension to the throne, but maintaining Cnut's laws was of vast importance to him, as it was during his regime that he acquired his wealth and position. More importantly, his support for Edward would keep him alive and secure. On the other hand, Edward could not afford to do anything drastic with Godwine. After all, the earl was still the most powerful and wealthiest noble in the land, and he had amassed a lot of local support as a figure who served all three Danish kings. Edward, on the other hand, had been an exile for a quarter of a century; he was effectively a stranger to his new subjects. Equally important was the fact that Godwine married a Danish noblewoman and that his issue wasn't purely Anglo-Saxon. That might not seem like an important detail, but with those blood ties, Godwine could technically raise a rebellion and have the Danish back him, both in England and across the sea in Scandinavia.

Until Harthacnut's death in 1042, Edward was a co-regent who was touted as the "king's brother." By that time, he had managed to earn the trust of some of his people, so much so that contemporary sources claim that there was a celebration of Edward's ascension before Harthacnut's body was even buried. His coronation took place on April 3rd, 1043, at Winchester Cathedral. Very early on, Edward tried to consolidate power and restore the old, traditional "strong" monarchy. He did so by first depriving his mother Emma and her steward, Stigard, of their property, citing the fact that she hadn't done enough to vouch for his succession, which was true. Soon enough, though, both were restored to their positions under Edward, and Emma would live until 1052.

Godwine's position continued to blossom under Edward despite the tensions. In 1043, the king appointed an earldom in the southwestern Midlands to Godwine's older son Sweyn. Two years later, on January 23rd, Godwine's family would become bound by marriage to Edward, with the king wedding the earl's daughter Edith. In addition, Godwine's younger son, Harold, received some lands, as did a Danish noble by the name of Beorn Estrithson. The entirety of southern England was now in some way under the control of either Godwine, his family members, or people related to Cnut who were loyal supporters of the earl. Sweyn would prove to be an unruly earl; he abducted the abbess of Leominster and was banished for this act in 1047. Both Harold and Beorn opposed his return in 1049, having split his territories amongst themselves, but Sweyn retaliated by murdering Beorn and fleeing again, with Beorn's lands going to Edward's nephew, Ralph the Timid. Sweyn would have remained in exile had Godwine not intervened and helped him get reinstated.

Other events marked Edward's early reign. Between 1045 and 1046, there was an imminent danger of Magnus the Good invading England and taking the throne. While Edward was initially ready for battle, he decided against helping one of Magnus's enemies, Sweyn II Estridsson. Sweyn was the cousin of Beorn and the son of Ulf, giving him a legitimate claim to the throne of Denmark. He waged war against Magnus with the help of Magnus's uncle, Harald Hardrada. The war ended with Magnus recognizing Harald as the co-ruler of Norway, and the king's death in 1047 officially prevented any potential invasion of England from happening. It had proven to be a wise move not to interfere, and Edward had spared his armies a pointless war against Magnus.

Edward's court did not entirely consist of Anglo-Saxon men. In fact, he allowed a few Normans to rise to power, much to the chagrin of the local nobles. Possibly the most prominent Norman to reach any position of power under Edward was Robert of Jumièges. Robert had been an abbot at Jumièges near Rouen in around 1037, and even back then, he had expressed support for Edward, which had earned him significant favors when the Confessor was officially made king. In 1044, Robert was the bishop of London, and a mere seven years later, he was raised to the rank of archbishop of Canterbury. During his time in office, he would often clash with Earl Godwine, and the feud between them would directly lead to their deaths, a succession crisis in England, and, inevitably, the advance of Duke William of Normandy in 1066.

Robert was not appointed the archbishop arbitrarily or because he was one of Edward's personal favorites. Earl Godwine had actually suggested a different bishop for promotion, but Edward vehemently refused. To add insult to injury, Robert kept accusing Godwine of illegal possession of certain church estates, which the archbishop from Jumièges would later try to "reclaim" for himself. However, this wasn't the event that pushed Godwine over the edge and into open rebellion against the king. That event happened a little later, with the arrival of Eustace II of Boulogne in England. Eustace's men had caused some trouble with the locals in Dover, and King Edward ordered Godwine to punish them for their transgression. Godwine, however, took the side of the Dovorians and refused to punish them, with his sons Harold and Sweyn taking his side. The Confessor saw this as the golden opportunity to take the earl and his family down a peg. With the help of Earls Siward and Leofric, Edward deprived Earl Godwine and his sons of their lands and exiled them in September of 1051. In addition, he sent Godwine's sister, Queen Edith, to a nunnery, routing every single member of the House of Godwine from any political position of power in England.

Godwine, his eldest son Sweyn, his wife Gytha, and his other two sons, Tostig and Gyrth, all fled to Flanders, while Harold and Godwine's other son, Leofwine, fled to Dublin. However, the very next year, the Godwines returned, ready to fight King Edward with a sizable army. Having learned of this course of events, Archbishop Robert fled England and crossed the Channel to get to Normandy. He was outlawed as a criminal, with Archbishop Stigand acting as his replacement. This event was controversial since Stigand had been both the bishop of Winchester and the archbishop of Canterbury, and the deposed Robert made sure to relay this information to Pope Leo IX, who (alongside multiple popes who followed) excommunicated Stigand for pluralism. Robert himself died at Jumièges, sometime between 1053 and 1055.

The story of Robert of Jumièges is vital to that of William the Conqueror. Reportedly, during his exile in Normandy, Robert met up with William and informed him that Edward, who was childless at the time, had named him as the successor to the throne. Whether or not this was true is up for debate, though it does sound plausible; after all, Robert was a native of Jumièges, making him well acquainted with every noble at the time and especially with William. And as a member of the clergy with Norman ties, he was familiar with William's military successes, as well as the family ties between the Norman duke and the English king. Nevertheless, William's conquest in 1066 wasn't solely because of Edward's supposed wish for the duke to succeed him. The other, equally important reason was the treatment of Robert at the hands of Godwine's men. William saw Robert's exile as the catalyst to invade England and take the throne from Godwine's successor, Harold.

Upon their return, both Godwine and his son Harold regained their old earldoms, and Edith was restored from the nunnery. Godwine's oldest son Sweyn went to Jerusalem for a pilgrimage but died upon his return, leaving Harold as the heir of Godwine's estates. He would come to claim them soon, for, on April 15th, 1053, Earl Godwine of Wessex died.

Sources claim that it was a sudden death, with some Norman apologists claiming that it was divine intervention and punishment for his involvement in the death of Alfred the Noble. Modern scholars find it more likely that he died of a stroke or a different type of sudden illness. With his passing, Harold took control of Wessex, and while his family was in shambles after the events of 1051, he would work hard to restore their reputation. In the following years, his surviving younger brothers—Gyrth, Leofwine, and Tostig—were given their own earldoms: East Anglia, Mercia, and Northumbria, respectively. As the years went on, the Godwinsons would reclaim their reputation among the English, with the only thorn in their side being Tostig.

Edward's rule between 1053 and 1066 was largely focused on skirmishes with Scotland and Wales. One of the men Edward supported was Malcolm, the son of the late King Duncan I. While Malcolm was an exile in England, Scotland was ruled by Macbeth, the same king who would come to be the main character of one of William Shakespeare's best-known tragedies. Edward helped Malcolm kill Macbeth and secure the throne by 1059, but the new Scottish king began to raid Northumbria as early as 1061, as he had expansionist tendencies.

In 1053, Welsh Prince Rhys ap Rhydderch was assassinated on King Edward's orders. Two years later, another noble, Gruffydd ap Llywelyn, rose to prominence as the king of all Wales. Allied with the outlawed Earl Ælfgar of Mercia, he began to raid the kingdom, which prompted Harold to gather a vast army to try to suppress the Welsh attackers. Gruffydd remained the king of the Welsh from 1057 to his death in 1063, swearing fealty to Edward in exchange for the Confessor recognizing his dominion over the territory of Wales. Soon after the death of Ælfgar, Gruffydd's most powerful ally, in early 1062, Harold and Tostig launched an attack on Gruffydd, pushing him farther into Welsh territory. King Gruffydd probably met his end in Snowdonia, either killed in combat or murdered by some of the locals. The second option seems more plausible; in his process of uniting the Welsh, Gruffydd definitely made some enemies along the way, so an assassination isn't entirely out of the question. With his death, Harold and Tostig imposed vassalage on some of the remaining princes of Wales.

The last major event to happen during Edward the Confessor's lifetime was the rebellion of the Northumbrian thegns against Tostig during one of his hunts in 1065. Tostig was one of the least favorite earls in the Confessor's kingdom, but his deposition and eventual exile were not simply based on his popularity. In all likelihood, Harold Godwinson wanted his brother out of the picture because he wanted to unite England. Tostig fled England, taking refuge with Baldwin V of Flanders, who was his brother-in-law. From there, Tostig would try every possible tactic to get back at Harold, especially when he took the throne after Edward's death. He raided the coast as far as Sandwich, tried to involve both Baldwin V and Norwegian King Harald Hardrada to join him (which Hardrada eventually did), had spent some time with King Malcolm III of Scotland in the summer of 1066, and even tried to form an alliance with Duke William himself. None of these acts would help him beat his brother, as Harold Godwinson would crush the united forces of Tostig and Hardrada at the famous Battle of Stamford Bridge, a mere two weeks before Duke William's advance at Hastings.

Edward fell ill by the end of December 1065. Evidently, he wanted Tostig protected and the rebellion squashed, but he had to submit to Harold and the thegns' demands and officially exile Tostig. This event might have led to a series of strokes, which left the king weak and frail. He was supposed to attend the dedication of a new church at Westminster on December 28th, when it was still undergoing construction, but was unable due to his frailty.

At some point, Edward had spoken to Harold, naming him as the heir to the throne in case of his demise. Soon after, on January 5th, Edward the Confessor died, with his burial taking place the next day at Westminster Abbey. On that same day, Harold Godwinson was crowned king by the Witan, starting the very short, very turbulent reign of the House of Godwinson.

An authentic sealed writ of Edward the Confessor, issued in favor of Westminster Abbey
https://commons.wikimedia.org/wiki/File:Edward_the_Confessor_sealed_writ.jpg

Prelude to the Conquest: Events in Normandy between 1057 and 1066

Written sources don't offer too many concrete details on William's activities between 1057 and 1060, though there are a few key details we can piece together based on what we do know. In early 1058, William had started invading the territory of the County of Dreux, taking over two important fortresses: Tillières and Thimert. Medieval writers such as Orderic Vitalis claim that there was a meeting at Fécamp that involved the duke, Bishop Lesceline of Paris, and Bishop Fulk of Amiens. The two bishops were on a peace mission from King Henry I, and supposedly, as an act of goodwill and an effort to maintain peace, the French king had gifted Duke William Tillières, which had been in his possession since the early 1040s. However, with William's takeover of Thimert, King Henry was convinced that he needed to take action, so he besieged the castle. Ralph IV, Count of Valois, provided help to Henry in 1058, as did Count Theobald III of Blois a year later, who was less than thrilled to do it and even less cooperative on the battlefield. William's forces managed to hold the line for the next two years, with William himself traveling around the country and performing other ducal duties.

Interestingly, the year 1060 would prove to be the best possible year for William's military exploits. William besieged a few more castles, namely Saint-Céneri-le-Gérei and La Roche-Mabile, both under Robert Fitz Giroie. Robert would die on February 6th, 1060, allowing his nephew, Arnold d'Echauffour, to succeed him in other matters. It should be noted that William was handling this siege at the same time King Henry was going after Thimert, showing that the duke was confident in waging war on two separate fronts.

Of course, 1060 was a year that just kept on giving. After a siege that looked more and more like a stalemate, King Henry I of France died on August 4th. The man who had proven to be both one of William's supporters and one of his most bitter enemies was no more; the siege of Thimert would be the last interaction the two men shared. And then November 14th rolled around, and the other bitter enemy of William who had been an ally of Henry, Count Geoffrey Martel of Anjou, passed away as well. Henry's successor, Philip I, was only eight years at that point, and two individuals would take it upon themselves to act as his regents. One was his mother, Queen Anne of Kiev, who had actually named the boy (Greek names like "Philip" were uncommon among western European leaders). In fact, she would become the first queen in the history of France to act as a regent, as well as the first Russian queen to have any semblance of power in France.

However, the other individual who became a regent for young Philip was far more important for both William and Normandy in general. Count Baldwin had been an interesting figure, supporting both the Norman troops and the invading Scandinavian armies, as well as the Danish claimants to the throne of England. Baldwin serving as the regent to the king of France might have posed a threat to William had the two been enemies. However, Baldwin's regency was actually going to work in William's favor, considering that the count's daughter was none other than William's wife, Matilda, who had already borne several children to William.

Both of William's bitterest rivals were now dead. The future king of France was in the hands of one of the duke's most trusted men. Duke William had not only strengthened the core of his country but had also managed to add more territory to it. And all throughout the course of these two years, he had been gifting monasteries, signing charters, and even founding the abbeys at Caen with his wife, Matilda. The resulting peace that was signed between Philip I and Duke William would result in a ten-year period of zero French-Norman conflicts, once again underlining the duke's ability to maintain peace in and around Normandy. After the previous decade had proven to be dreadful and mired with a mixture of successes and failures (though successes overwhelmingly prevailed), the year 1060 could well be remembered as the best period of William's life until the events of 1066.

Conquest of Maine

Maine was a province south of Normandy, and it was ruled by its own counts. It was located right on the border of another county that had been locked in constant conflict with William: Anjou. During the 1050s, Maine was under the control of the Angevines, with Geoffrey Martel being in charge after a successful invasion. At the time, the ruler of Maine was Count Herbert II, the son of the late Hugh IV, who had died in 1051. Herbert had fled to Normandy in 1056, seeking William's help. The two men then arranged a marriage between William's firstborn son Robert and Herbert's sister Marguerite. However, the countess would later die without ever marrying. Aside from betrothing their children, the duke and the count had arranged another marriage agreement, wherein William's daughter Adelida was to marry Herbert. This marriage wasn't going to be any more fruitful than the other one, as Herbert died in 1062, leaving Maine in a succession crisis. The crisis would have been complicated enough had Herbert not declared William his heir in Maine in case of his death, a declaration that the duke was more than happy to put into practice.

Prior to any business with Maine, William was struck by a serious illness that was nearly fatal. Sources aren't clear on what exactly the illness was, when he contracted it, where he contracted it, or when exactly he got better, but based on the political situation in Maine and other surrounding states, as well as William's activity regarding the churches, it's safe to say that the whole event took place in the very early 1060s, with William getting better possibly as soon as early 1062.

Even if we don't take late Herbert's declaration of a new heir into account, Maine had been one of William's goals since the 1050s, as well as a bitter memory of events that had happened in the not-so-distant past. Geoffrey Martel had invaded the region back in the day, and the influence of Geoffrey of Mayenne was also still strongly felt. But with the deaths of both Martel and King Henry I, the House of Anjou, which was effectively the overlord of Maine, was no longer a major threat to William. Seizing the opportunity, William moved in to take the county. Aside from the declaration of Herbert, the duke of Normandy had also claimed the title over Maine using the marriage of his son Robert and the late Herbert's sister Marguerite, the one that hadn't come to fruition. Naturally, William wasn't the only claimant, with at least one more contender raising to the spotlight: Count Walter III of Vexin.

Walter was the son of Drogo of Vexin, a powerful count who had, at one point, married Goda, the daughter of Æthelred the Unready. That combination alone made Walter a dangerous man since he could, according to the complicated rules of succession laid out several paragraphs ago, potentially have laid claim to both Normandy and England. The reasoning he used to claim Maine largely revolved around his marriage to Biota, the sister of Hugh IV of Maine. For a brief period of time, it seemed like Walter was going to hold onto some of the lands in Maine, as they had sworn fealty to him. In addition, he enjoyed the support of both Geoffrey of Mayenne and one Hubert de Sainte-Suzanne, Vicomte of Le Mans. But most importantly, he had the support of Geoffrey the Bearded, Martel's oldest son, who had succeeded him on the throne of Anjou. Of course, that support wasn't going to last for long since Geoffrey was in a succession dispute with his younger brother, Fulk IV, whom history remembers by the nickname *le Réchin*, meaning "surly" or "quarrelsome" due to his supposed nasty habits and poor behavior. With the Angevines in a full-on civil war, William knew it was the perfect opportunity to snatch Maine, which he did at some point in 1063.

His takeover of Maine had been his most methodical and careful military campaign yet, and as a seasoned warrior, he implemented every single tactic for which he had become known. Initially, he would gather his allies carefully, reminding them of old fealties, slowly building an army to overcome his opponent. William, at that time, was never one to rush into battle, even if the opportunity for it was golden. The death of Geoffrey

Martel was the event that tipped the scales in his favor, and by all accounts, Geoffrey the Bearded was nowhere near as assertive as a leader or as clever of a tactician as his father had been. But even then, and especially during the dispute between the two Angevine brothers, William bided his time. Most of his troop-gathering was probably done in the spring of 1063.

With enough men at his command, William would begin his takeover, but he wouldn't attack with a full-scale assault. Instead, he slowly raided the local villages and areas, demoralizing the locals enough to either scare them into submission or weed out the problematic ones. By doing this, he tightened the noose around Le Mans and avoided full-on warfare with either the people of Maine or their overlords, the Angevines. Attacking the city directly, even with an army that was twice that of Maine and Anjou combined, would have resulted in devastating losses of life on both sides.

Both Walter and Biota surrendered to William, either willingly before he reached Le Mans or during the takeover of the castle itself. Some sources place them at Falaise during their supposed submission to William, and in August of that same year, they would both die suddenly and under unexplained circumstances. Most medieval authors, like Orderic, usually categorize every sudden and unexplained death of a noble as foul play, most often citing poisoning as the reason behind their demise. And in William's time, poisoning wasn't exactly uncommon among the members of the nobility, even at the lower end of the aristocratic spectrum. But there might have been a more plausible explanation for the quick demise of Walter and Biota. If they were at Falaise, they must have surrendered to William directly, after which he could have had them imprisoned. William was particularly notorious for treating his prisoners in the most horrific, ruthless ways imaginable, even if the prisoners had committed comparably minor offenses to the ones of

Walter and his wife. It's highly likely that the two either succumbed to the torture performed on them in the dungeons or to the consequences of spending time in captivity under William.

William's entry at Le Mans saw the people surrendering left and right, with the members of the clergy swearing fealty to William. In another prudent move, the duke did not take massive swathes of territory from the local nobles and distribute them to the Normans under his service. Instead, he tried his best to maintain the status quo, interfering in a substantial enough way for the people of Maine to stay loyal to him. This collaborative approach would prove to be a success, considering the fact that the bishop of Le Mans would provide him with ships during his campaign to England.

But Le Mans wasn't the only castle William would take during his Maine campaign. One final fort remained, and it was the elusive, daunting castle of Mayenne, where Geoffrey still resided. William decided to raid this castle by setting it on fire first, which caused panic among the locals living there. Upon entering the castle, the duke allowed his troops to raid and pillage everything in sight; everything they took would be theirs as a reward for their service. The takeover of Mayenne again showed two more crucial bits of William's tactics, one of which had been in practice for centuries before his birth, while the other was mostly his own "signature style." Gifting soldiers, generals, and allies with the spoils of war was a time-honored tradition of the Middle Ages, as it would give the troops incentive to keep fighting for a ruler, even if the odds were against them. In addition, there was always a good chance that a soldier could rise through the ranks and become a noble or even buy his way into nobility with the spoils he would earn during a raid. On the other hand, there was the violence and ruthlessness of William's warfare, even after the battle had been won. Violent behavior toward the losing side was nothing new in medieval western Europe, but William seemed to have brought it up to a whole new level, as he was especially cruel during strategically important battles, such as the one at Mayenne. In fact, his conduct was so brutal that even some of his most ardent supporters who wrote about his life had to admit to the sheer savagery of the deaths and tortures they had witnessed, and they would often struggle to justify his brutality and decontextualize it to fit their image of a just and fair ruler who did what was right.

Interestingly, Geoffrey of Mayenne did not perish with the takeover of his castle. What's more, he hadn't really lost his land to begin with, meaning that William probably did the same with him as he did with the other nobles of Maine—left him in charge while forcing him to swear fealty to the Norman crown. Geoffrey, as the clear loser of this battle, most likely had to swallow his pride and accept William's seniority, but the two would never be on good terms.

After the fighting was done, William had Marguerite transferred to be brought up at the court, effectively being raised to marry his son Robert when they were both of age. However, she died there soon after and was buried alongside the rest of the ducal family at Fécamp. William also normalized his relations with Count Ralph of Valois, the man who had taken over both Amiens and Vexin, thus becoming the heir of the late Count Walter. Ralph was one of William's opponents during the Battle of Mortemer, and this change of allegiance showed both William's propensity to pardon his enemies and the shifting tides in contemporary politics in northern France during the 1060s. William's son Robert apparently had to do homage as well, swearing fealty to Geoffrey the Bearded, with the duke himself being a witness of this event. This event was not done under any sense of duty that William might have had toward Count Geoffrey (after all, it was Geoffrey who lost the war and William who held Maine). Rather, it was another in the long line of prudent moves that would bring the elite of Maine and the surrounding states closer to that of Normandy, which was now the effective overlord of the region.

As the new ruler of Maine, William was an arbiter of several court disputes between 1063 and 1066, with him ruling in favor of one abbey, apparently doing so by imposing his decision rather than carefully overviewing the entirety of the case itself. This action can either be seen as William not having the patience to go over the case and simply using Occam's razor to make a decision (the abbey he ruled against had no evidence to support they were given the land that was the subject of the dispute) or as a quick-witted decision based on a genuine and objective overview of the evidence. On the other hand, it could have simply been the duke's desire to assert his dominance by proving himself an arbiter who had the final word. However, during a different dispute following the death of Bishop Wulgrin of Le Mans and the subsequent appointment of Bishop Arnold from Avranchin to the position, William did not interfere and allowed the clergy to settle the matter, which they did.

It would barely be three years before William would set off for England, and he already was a force to be reckoned with. Having either crushed or subdued his former enemies, the duke had inarguably become the biggest player in northern France, with his influence perhaps rivaling that of the French kings in the past century. With the conquest of Maine, he had secured Normandy's southern border and brought Anjou to heel, a feat that served both as a necessary political maneuver and a personal victory based on his past experiences with the prominent men of these lands. However, William wasn't quite done with consolidating his power in western Europe. He still had his western borders to strengthen, a feat that, based on his string of successful campaigns, could only end in one way.

The Campaign in Brittany

During William's period of power consolidation, Brittany was ruled by Duke Conan II of Rennes. Conan's immediate ancestors had a history with William and Normandy in the past, with the two non-French duchies (Brittany was predominantly Celtic, while Normandy was made up of assimilated Norsemen) maintaining relations that were often amicable but frequently tended to turn tense. For instance, Conan's father had been none other than Count Alan III, who had died in 1040, fighting by William's side. Conan's uncle, Count Eudo, had initially been on William's side but had decided to support Geoffrey Martel at Ambrières. He had also ruled Brittany as a regent when seven-year-old Conan was declared the heir. Eudo effectively held his nephew hostage until 1057 when Conan, now an adult, captured Eudo and chained him up in a cell. William's subsequent advance on Brittany might have had something to do with Eudo's abandonment at Ambrières, but the more likely reason was the duke's support of Rivallon of Dol, a rebel who had risen against Conan in an attempt to expand his territories. Rivallon and William had prior connections, with the former receiving some land as a result of the abbey territorial dispute William had resolved not long ago. In fact, it might have been William who had convinced Rivallon to rebel in the first place.

The Brittany campaign of 1064 is quite interesting not because of its outcome, which historians are still unsure of (though it was more than likely that William came to an agreement with Conan in the end), but because of who participated in it. Aside from Duke William and Lord Rivallon, the invaders were joined by Geoffrey the Bearded of Anjou (though this is contested by some authors of that era), as well as, of all people, Harold Godwinson. Harold was in Normandy at that time for reasons that aren't fully known to modern historians. Some scribes, possibly as a part of pro-Norman propaganda, wrote that Harold had specifically come to discuss William's ascension to the throne of England with him, with the legend stating that the future king of England had broken his oath, which caused William to righteously march into war against the English. However, Harold was more than likely hunting or fishing along the English coast, and his ship was caught in a storm and ended up on the European shore. Alternatively, he might have been seeking his exiled family members who were driven out of the country during King Edward the Confessor's early reign. Whatever the case might have been, Harold had a tumultuous few years on mainland Europe, having been captured by Guy of Ponthieu and then handed over to William. The two nobles would lead a joint campaign against Conan II, joining forces with Rivallon of Dol.

The invaders first struck Dol, which made Conan retreat to Rennes and then the Dinan castle. Supposedly, Conan surrendered here, though some sources claim he enlisted the help of Geoffrey the Bearded, who responded promptly. This, alongside Rivallon's supposed claim that the campaign had left his land ravaged, may have actually caused William to retreat, despite having the upper hand, and reach an agreement with Conan.

The true course of events of the Brittany campaign is not well known, but based on the outcome, they hint strongly at a truce and the future cooperation between Brittany and Normandy. For instance, Conan confirmed a grant to an abbey that was given by Rivallon prior to the rebellion, and moreover, he reconfirmed it to Rivallon's surviving family members after his death sometime in 1065. In addition, Conan would invade Anjou in 1066, presumably on William's behalf, where he took the castles of Pouancé and Segré. His mysterious death at Château-Gontier, unsurprisingly linked to poisoning, on December 11th, 1066, was attributed to Duke William, as sources believe the Norman ruler had Conan's riding gloves laced with poison. Conan was succeeded by his sister, Duchess Hawise of Rennes, and her husband Hoël II, the former Count of Kernev.

Overall, the Brittany campaign might appear to be a waste of resources and a completely pointless exercise, at least when compared to the former campaigns of Maine, Varaville, or Mortemer. After all, William had no need to conquer Brittany, nor did he have to show his support of a minor lord rebelling in someone else's duchy. Modern historians call this campaign the perfect example of "political theater," and that's precisely what it had been. The goal of William's advance into Brittany was to secure Normandy's borders; that much is true. But in reality, the Norman duke simply wanted to maintain a firm grip on his neighbors, which would help him instill loyalty and fealty in them. As a result, he would have them on his side during major campaigns, like the one that would happen across the Channel a mere few years after his dealings with Conan and Rivallon. Some Bretons directly supported William's cause, but more importantly, they became an important ally when it came to maintaining a grip on power in northern France. And bringing Harold along as an ally was a stroke of genius; despite Godwine's death, his immediate family was still the richest and most powerful in England, and Harold was still a close, prominent advisor to King Edward. Not only was this an excellent show of support from a powerful ally across the sea, but it would also provide William with a plausible line of reasoning behind his supposed election to be the heir of the Confessor. William's military prowess had proven itself once again in practice, and whether he had won the Brittany campaign or not is irrelevant. The war against Conan had achieved exactly what the duke needed, and now, he was ready to take on the biggest challenge of his life.

1066: The Battle of Hastings

By the time Harold had been crowned king in early 1066, he had both met and fought alongside William of Normandy. More importantly, as the direct descendant of Godwine, he was well aware of the influence the Normans had at the English court during Edward the Confessor's reign. Harold knew this Norman influence had directly impacted his family's good fortune, as the actions of Robert of Jumièges would have been fresh in the king's memory. Harold also knew that there were several contenders to the throne of England, with some more legitimate than others.

Possibly the most legitimate candidate to return to England and attempt to take the throne was Edgar Ætheling, the late Confessor's grandnephew. Edgar's father, known as Edward the Exile, had spent nearly his whole adult life in exile at the Hungarian court, having been driven out of the country when Cnut came to power. Since the Confessor had no issue, he summoned Edward back to England, but Edward the Exile died in 1057, mere days after arriving in England. At the time, Edgar had only been six years old, and he was barely even considered as a potential successor. Whether Edward the Confessor wanted his grandnephew to succeed him during the years between Edward the Exile's death and his own passing in 1066 is not exactly known to history, though there are some clues to this option at least being considered. Edgar had received his epithet Ætheling, "the trustworthy," upon his arrival and subsequent upbringing at the English court. Ætheling had been an epithet of several figures in English history, and the term itself also designated princes, i.e., heirs to English kings. Even without the epithet, we have other hints that the Confessor might have, at least initially, considered Edgar as his heir. One such act was Edgar's court upbringing, which could be seen as Edward simply taking care of his extended family, but it's not unlikely that he was preparing his grandnephew to take the throne.

Of course, when we take into account the events between 1057, when Edward the Exile died, and 1066, when the Confessor's death occurred, there's a massive nine-year gap that makes barely any mentions of Edgar as an heir. King Edward must have shifted his focus from his minor grandnephew to the Godwinson family, who had been slowly regaining their lost reputation. Nearly all great nobles at the time, including Harold and William, claimed that Edward had bestowed the throne upon them in case he died without issue, but in terms of sheer plausibility, Harold Godwinson might have actually received Edward's direct support. It is true the two men were not exactly on friendly terms, considering that Edward had wronged Godwine on numerous occasions before and that Godwine's support of Edward had been opportunistic at best. However, in Edward's eyes, Harold would have been the most logical and most stable choice. Harold enjoyed the support of many nobles, a fact that is made clear with how quickly the Witan chose him as the successor after the Confessor died. On the other hand, Edgar had no real support within England, nor did he have the military to back up his claim. In addition, he was only fifteen when his granduncle died. This fact would not have prevented him from taking the throne by any means, but in terms of military prowess, political insight, and influence, he was no match for his senior superiors like Harold.

However, young Ætheling was just one of the claimants to the English crown. By this point, William had made it no secret that he was aiming for the throne at Westminster, and he had been preparing for a full-scale assault years before Harold ascended to kingship. In addition, King Harald Hardrada of Norway claimed the throne. His claim was based on an agreement between Harthacnut and Magnus, wherein if the son of Cnut died without issue, Magnus would take power. However, with

Magnus dying in the meantime, Harald took up the claim and started preparing for an invasion. Between 1064 and his death in 1066, Harald had been the king of Norway, relinquishing his dominion over Denmark to Sweyn II. Interestingly, Sweyn was another claimant to the English throne, mostly through his familial relations to Cnut (thus giving him a better claim than Harald's), though he wouldn't turn his attention to England until after the 1066 Conquest.

The final major claimant was, of course, Duke William of Normandy. If contemporary sources are to be believed, he had several reasons to claim the throne. Firstly, his mother, Emma, had given birth to two English kings: Edward the Confessor and Harthacnut. Next, there was the treatment of Robert of Jumièges by the English, specifically the Godwinsons. And finally, the two key reasons behind William's claim all had to do with the legal "transfer" of succession onto him by prominent figures in England, more specifically Edward and Harold themselves.

Of course, William's claims, when we look at them through a critical lens, were flimsy at best and can even be seen as a justification of what was essentially a hostile takeover. When Harold ascended to power, everyone, from the Danish to the Norwegians to the Normans, wanted to try their hand at the English crown, and they all went about it in different ways.

Preparing for the Battle

It would be an understatement to claim that both Harold and William were preparing for their inevitable clash, but what is often overlooked is the third man that would play a major impact on the events of 1066. Harold's brother Tostig had only recently been exiled, an act that had earned Harold even more support with the English. Tostig, as stated earlier, did not take this lying down, and he allied himself with Harald Hardrada and was ready to fight his way back to England.

Harold was aware of Tostig's exploits during most of early 1066, but his immediate concern was Duke William. During the summer, the king assembled an impressive fleet at Sandwich and stationed it along the English coast, close to the Isle of Wight. He had managed to amass his troops in a surprisingly short amount of time, which goes some way to show that he was, without a doubt, the popular choice for the kingship among the English nobility.

William wasted no time in preparing for the invasion. He had been traveling across Normandy, granting charters in all of the prominent monasteries and churches (Fécamp, Caen, Rouen, Bayeux, and Bonneville-sur-Touques), and in nearly all of his visits, some of his most prominent supporters are listed as present. These included William Fitz Osbern, Roger II of Montgomery, Roger of Beaumont, William's half-brothers Odo of Bayeux and Robert of Mortain, and William's wife Matilda and their firstborn son Robert. At some point in early 1066, a council was held in the county of Lillebonne, where the major members of the Norman aristocracy most likely discussed the upcoming attack on the English. Around this time, William received the official papal banner from Pope Alexander II, effectively gaining permission from the Catholic Church to "justly invade" England. Alongside the banner, William had received the papal ring, as well as an edict directed to the Old English clergy with instructions to submit to William once he entered England. Alexander and William had maintained a solid relationship after the passing of the previous pope, so Alexander's permission and blessing for the attack on the English might have been more of a personal affair than a legal act.

Aside from his Norman subjects, William amassed an army of non-Norman nobles from the region, specifically from Boulogne and Brittany. The total number of William's forces isn't known, but the most accurate estimate is about 14,000 soldiers, roughly the same as the army Harold Godwinson had at his disposal. Some sources also claim that William enlisted a number of mercenaries, which wasn't uncommon at the time for any war-waging noble in western Europe. In addition, the duke ordered the construction of what amounted to be 3,000 ships, which might sound too good to be true at first glance. After all, the ship-builders at the time didn't have the sophisticated technology we have today. However, when we take into account that Tostig had managed to acquire 60 ships during a single winter from Flanders, 3,000 ships seem plausible if all of William's men were footing the bill and if they had from January 1066 to late summer of that same year to prepare. William's fleet was ready even earlier than that, and the original attack was supposed to take place on August 12th, but he decided against crossing the Channel during the summer, possibly due to the unstable waters and the harsh storms that tended to occur during that time of the year. In addition, Harold's fleet was stationed across the shore, and it only dispersed when Harold took some of his first victories against Harald Hardrada and his brother Tostig. With Harold gone in late September to face off the two in the north, William's fleet crossed the Channel, either on September 27th or 28th, during the night. Supposedly, they landed at Pevensey in Sussex, with a portion of the fleet being blown off course and landing at Romney, where they fought the local troops and were all slaughtered.

The Battle of Stamford Bridge

Harold Godwinson was in an incredibly unfavorable position. Tostig, whom he had exiled, had returned, joining forces with the Norwegians and raiding in the north of the country. Well aware of William's eventual landing in England, King Harold had to essentially fight a war on two fronts. In the north, Harald and Tostig defeated the English army in York, offering the Northumbrians peace if they provided them with hostages and acknowledged Harald as their king. The Northumbrians were then ordered to send additional hostages, as well as supplies, at Stamford Bridge, and when this information reached King Harold, he knew he had to act. With a massive army, he departed from London to Yorkshire, reaching it in an incredible four days and catching Harald's troops on September 25th completely by surprise.

The fighting between the two armies was fierce, with neither side letting up, but with the subsequent deaths of both Harald Hardrada and Tostig, the Norwegian troops began to scatter. Harold Godwinson had won the battle, though an additional charge was made by the late Hardrada's potential son-in-law, a noble by the name of Eystein Orre. He initially managed to put a dent in the English forces, but Harold eventually prevailed, with Orre dying in battle and his men ending up either scattered and drowning in the nearby rivers or dead on the battlefield.

The victory at Stamford Bridge was, by far, the absolute highlight of Harold's reign. He had successfully routed a strong enemy force and had secured England from further Norwegian advances by forcing Harald's son Olaf, a survivor of the battle, to pledge not to attack in the future. The few remaining Norwegian ships (sources claim that only twenty-four ships disembarked after the Battle of Stamford) took Olaf to the Orkney Islands, which was the earldom of Hardrada's ally and another survivor of the battle, Paul Thorfinnsson, who also took the same pledge as Olaf. It's unfortunate that King Harold would not live long to reap the accolades of this victory since he had to rally his troops right back south. William was advancing.

The Battle of Hastings

Upon his arrival at Pevensey, William ordered the construction of a wooden fort, which served as his temporary headquarters while he raided the nearby countryside. While at Hastings, William used an old Iron Age fort as his base of operations, continuing his pattern of looting and raiding the countryside, partly to crush the morale of the locals but partly due to the need to gain supplies and sustain his garrison. King Harold hurried south upon hearing of the raids, which might suggest that William had been just as ruthless and bloodthirsty as he normally was during his military exploits. Aside from raids, women were also taken as slaves or were sexually assaulted by the Norman soldiers, a gruesome yet standard practice of medieval warfare. The property had been so devastated that the value of land dropped significantly, even many years after the battle and during William's reign. In short, Harold had found the land utterly ravaged.

Harold might have wanted to launch a surprise attack on William, but the duke's Norman scouts spotted the king's army advancing long before he could do anything.

Emissaries might have been sent to vie for peace, something that William evidently refused. On the battlefield itself, on that fateful October 14th, the duke might have offered Harold a humiliating deal, wherein he would spare his life and allow him to rule over his father's old earldom in exchange for the crown. Even if this deal had been offered, Harold would have refused it. The battle was inevitable, and each side had its advantages. William had structured his army so that the Normans would be at the center, the Bretons on the left, and the French on the right. William himself was at the dead center of his own troops. The front line consisted of archers and crossbowmen, the back of heavy infantry, and the rear of cavalry. Harold, on the other hand, had taken the high ground, which would have made William's troops advance a steep slope. However, the position Harold's army was in was only accessible along a narrow isthmus, making an orderly retreat all but impossible, and furthermore, the English troops were extremely cramped, which made for poor maneuverability.

But their position all but ensured that William was not going to flank the English.

The charge began. Initially, no side gave any quarter to the other. The Norman coalition advanced harshly and brutally, possibly in short bursts, while the English stood fast and repelled nearly every advance. The battle started out early in the morning, around 9 a.m., and nobody knew back then that it would last well into dusk, making it one of the longest single battles of medieval history. William had ingeniously only advanced up the slope when there was a chance of Harold launching his own attack, thus slowly wearing the king's troops down while saving as much of his own soldiers' stamina as possible. At some point, it appeared as if William was going to lose, with the Bretons, in particular, being in a state of disarray. There were even rumors on the battlefield that William had died, which made his triumphant reemergence and brutal counter-advance all the more epic. Upon hearing of William's supposed death, the French started to kill the English soldiers with an added ferocity. Naturally, William's men were right there with him when he reemerged, including Count Eustace of Boulogne, who rushed right behind him, providing assistance. William had taken risks with solo outings, where he would mow down enemy after enemy, but the risks were calculated, and there would always be one or two of his men at his side protecting him. Two feigned retreats followed at one point, though it was unlikely that William had withdrawn all of his troops. More than likely, small garrisons would have broken off in a mock retreat for the English to follow, only to turn back and slaughter them when they were away from the main army. Sources claim that William killed Harold's brother Gyrth, and while the noble did die during the battle, his killer is still unknown to history.

Interestingly, we also aren't entirely sure how Harold lost his life during the battle. Most written accounts, which date decades after the battle, mention an arrow striking the king in the head, killing him instantly. One legend even has a random Norman soldier hacking the king's dead body only for William to punish him for disorderly and unchivalrous conduct. Whatever the case may be, Harold lost his life on the battlefield, as did his brothers Gyrth and Leofwine. William's troops would continue to slaughter the English well into the night, and the duke seems to have refused to spare anyone or take any prisoners. The battle was over, and the English had lost.

On the following day, written sources mention that William allowed the surviving English to bury their dead, but more importantly, he might have also allowed them to bury Harold. He was most likely buried at Waltham Holy Cross church, which he had founded and endowed during his life.

The Hastings Aftermath: Conquest of England and Coronation

After the battle, William launched a full-scale assault on the southeast of England, ravaging Sussex, Kent, Hampshire, Middlesex, and Hertfordshire. When he reached Romney, William was particularly cruel, massacring the troops and getting vengeance for the loss of his men during the landing. He then moved on to Dover, which surrendered due to a lack of confidence. At Dover, William's men were struck with dysentery, and there was even news that William had taken ill. Back in London, the prominent nobles decided on elevating Edgar Ætheling as king, and his claim was supported by all the prominent members of the clergy and nobility, including Harold's military commanders Earl Edwin and Earl Morcar (who had fought valiantly against Harald Hardrada mere months earlier), as well as Archbishops Stigand and Ealdred. One of William's detachments was sent to Winchester, which surrendered. Winchester was also the home of the Dowager Queen Edith, who surrendered to the new regime and was thus allowed to keep her lands.

With William now at London's front gates, raiding and pillaging around the area, the intimidation finally took root, and the inevitable surrender of the English nobles took place. Both Earls Edwin and Morcar, Bishops Walter of Hereford and Wulfstan of Worcester, Archbishop Ealdred, and the chief citizenry of London all bent the knee to William. Most importantly, Edgar Ætheling, a teenager who had been elevated to the new successor mere weeks prior, accepted his fate and acknowledged William as his sovereign. A few months later, on Christmas Day, 1066, William was crowned king. The Conqueror had achieved a monumental feat, which earned him an epithet that would go down in history. It was the dawn of a new era.

The Death of King Harold Godwinson, Bayeux Tapestry Scene 57
https://commons.wikimedia.org/wiki/File:Bayeux_Tapestry_scene57_Harold_death.jpg

Chapter 3 – From Duke to King: Ruling over England and Normandy

Early in his reign, King William gave lands in England to his closest collaborators, as well as the nobles who submitted to him early on. For instance, parts of Wessex and Kent were now under William Fitz Osbern and Bishop Odo of Bayeux. In early 1067, the newly crowned king sailed across the Channel back to Normandy, taking an entourage of English nobles with him (notably the ones who supported Edgar as the new king, such as Edwin and Morcar; Edgar himself was also a part of this entourage). While he was away, William put Fitz Osbern and Odo of Bayeux in charge of England, who were two of his most trusted men at that moment. During William's stay in Normandy, his former ally, Eustace of Boulogne, would lend a helping hand to the Kentish rebellion in Dover. Eustace was beaten by William's forces, and his lands were taken from him, resulting in his banishment. However, William would restore Eustace to power and give some of his lands back in a few years, possibly because he was too influential of an ally to dismiss.

The new king's allies also received lands after William's return to England, with each division of land going under the term "rape." Robert of Mortain gained the rape of Pevensey, Robert of Eu the rape of Hastings, and William of Warenne the rape of Lewes. Roger of Montgomery would gain two territories: Arundel and Chichester. Most of Godwine's native land, Sussex, was also heavily partitioned among William's followers.

Some battles ensued, with one of them being William's advance against the city of Exeter in 1067 in order to crush the rebellion of Eadric the Wild, a local lord. Eadric ravaged Harford before reaching Exeter, and Gytha, the mother of the late King Harold Godwinson, was a major part of this rebellion. A skirmish with Harold's surviving sons occurred, and they landed at Bristol from their new base in Ireland and raided southwestern England. Both the battle of Exeter and the fight against the supporters of late Harold went in William's favor.

With rebellions cropping up everywhere around England, William's subordinates (and soon enough, William himself) commissioned the building of various castles, which were placed strategically to keep the land in check. William Fitz Osbern was credited with building at least six castles (including Clifford Castle in his own earldom of Hereford and Carisbrooke Castle on the Isle of Wight), while William built them at Lincoln, Cambridge, and Huntingdon. Not only were they built as defensive structures and as barracks for the stationed troops, but they would also serve as a harsh reminder of who was in charge, thus putting a psychological strain on the people who lived nearby.

The next order of business was to crown Matilda as queen, something which William had no chance of doing while at Hastings a few years prior.

After her coronation, Matilda would become more involved in William's affairs in England, insofar as being present on nearly all signatures of English church diplomas at the time. However, for the majority of her tenure as queen, she was concentrated in Normandy. Her coronation took place at Winchester in May 1068.

William's tenure as king, from 1066 to his death on September 9th, 1087, was filled to the brim with events that go well beyond the scope of this book. This chapter will cover some of the most prominent events that shaped his reign and, more specifically, shaped the way ruling a cross-Channel kingdom worked in the Middle Ages.

Coin of William the Conqueror, 1066-1087
https://commons.wikimedia.org/wiki/File:William_the_Conqueror_1066_1087.jpg

The Maine Rebellion and the Harrying of the North

The period between 1069 and 1071 would prove to be one of the most troubling during William's early reign as king. There was an issue with maintaining the lands in the north, with one steward after another proving to be a problem. The first magnate of the north, Copsig, was in office for less than five weeks before he was killed by his immediate successor,

Osulf. Both men were, at some point, loyal to the regime of Harold Godwinson, and both would come to suffer the same fate, as Osulf was murdered not long after. He was replaced by his cousin, Gospatric, the man who would join Edgar Ætheling in a newly sparked rebellion against the Norman king. As his replacement, the ruling regime appointed a Norman called Robert of Comines.

The rebels who supported Edgar's rekindled claim to the throne started by raiding the northern lands. Robert of Comines decided to meet them in early 1069 and rode to Durham, but both he and his men were mercilessly slaughtered. The rebels, emboldened by their successes, took the castle of York, but they would not hold it for long. William, who was in England at the time, swiftly rode to the city and drove the rebels out, killing vast numbers of them in the process. Edgar's forces fled to Scotland, though they were far from finished with their plans.

A series of small rebellions in the Midlands, as well as in the south (Shrewsbury, Dorset, and Devon), forced William to move his attention away from the north. He rallied his troops to the Midlands while his earls handled the other areas. At this point, King Sweyn II of Denmark sent ships and troops to support Edgar Ætheling. The combined forces of the English and the Danish recaptured York, and once again, William's return and recapture of the city was swift, though this time, he didn't have to wage war—instead, the rebels fled York, with Edgar departing for Scotland, yet again to the court of King Malcolm. According to some sources, William sacked York nonetheless and then sent for his crown to be brought to him all the way from Winchester. He supposedly wore the crown in the ruins of York as a show of his victory over the Danes.

The beaten Danish, tired and facing the harsh winter in the north, came to an agreement with King William. He would pay their commander, Earl Osbjorn, a large sum of money and allowed him to raid some of the local lands for supplies under the condition that the Danes abandoned England and not fight the Crown anymore. The event took place in early 1070, and it would be followed by one of the worst atrocities in medieval English history ever attributed to William.

With the Danes gone, William focused on the rebels of the north. He split his army into small regimens and had them essentially carpet-bomb the region with some of the vilest acts imaginable. William's men murdered thousands of people, both those guilty of rebelling and those who had nothing to do with it. In addition to the murders, displacements were common, and some of the refugees from these actions ended up as far as the West Midlands, close to Wales. Entire villages were burned to the ground, raided, or torn apart in merciless ways. Livestock was butchered, and food storages were either decimated or raided. It was the winter of 1070, so food was already scarce, but William's troops made sure that nothing remained so that the rebels (and anyone else, really) would starve to death. There were even reports of the locals resorting to cannibalism due to the famine that ensued, a famine that would take the lives of a projected 100,000 people. The effects of this event, known as the Harrying of the North, were felt decades into William's reign and even after his death. Scholars treat this event as a genocide, citing William's potential distrust of the English, a distrust that would only grow stronger after the series of rebellions that took place up to and including the one at York. However, William was shown to provide leniency to the English who submitted to his rule, despite giving all of the earldoms to people from the mainland (a practice that would be applied full-scale once William returned to the south after the Harrying).

During William's stay in England, a revolt took place in Maine, more than likely orchestrated by Geoffrey of Mayenne, an old enemy of the king. While most of the king's important members of the elite were in

England, helping to consolidate power, the rebels, who had huge support from the people of Maine, chased all of William's supporters out of Le Mans and established themselves there. Mayenne's collaborators during this rebellion were Azzo d'Este II, the margrave ("count") of Milan, his wife Gersendis, and their son Hugh, later to be known as Hugh V. While their unity was questionable and would soon fracture, they managed to take the castle when none of William's main men were there to protect it. The Manceaux people declared Hugh as their count, but he proved to be an ineffective leader, selling off his position to his cousin Elias I in 1092.

The Early 1070s and William's First Losses

While William was still in England, Flanders underwent a crisis. Count Baldwin VI, Queen Matilda's brother, had died in July 1070, and their brother, Robert (later known as Robert the Frisian), would become the next contender for the throne, challenging Baldwin's widow Richilde, who was acting as regent for the late count's son and rightful heir, Arnulf III. Fearing for her position, the countess sought help from one of William's most important allies, William Fitz Osbern, offering him her hand in marriage. Wanting to attain power over Flanders, and most likely to subdue the situation in Flanders, Fitz Osbern joined Arnulf's supporters, alongside a sizable French regiment sent by King Philip I. The forces would meet at the Battle of Cassel on February 22nd, 1071, which would end up being a decisive victory for Robert and elevate him as the count of Flanders. Both Arnulf III and William Fitz Osbern lost their lives in combat.

Around the same time, somewhere between 1070 and 1071, tragedy would strike William's household when his son, Richard, died in a hunting accident. The exact cause of death isn't known, though some sources from the time claim he was hit in the head by an overhead branch. Though he was not William's oldest son, Richard still showed promise, making his death all the more tragic.

Both the situation at Flanders, with the loss of his most trusted companion, and the news of his son's accidental death most likely weighed heavily on William on a personal level. However, the ramifications were much more severe. The situations at Flanders and Maine showed that even William's power and influence had limits, as well as one other crucial detail—governing both lands at once would require a lot more effort with a lot more engagement from both the king and his surviving subjects.

The Siege of Ely

As early as 1070, the Danish would pose a new problem for William, with King Sweyn raiding the eastern shores. He would eventually reach the Isle of Ely and join forces with Hereward (later to be known as "Hereward the Wake"), a local thegn who opposed William's regime. While William managed to reach an agreement with Sweyn, after which the Danish king took his troops back to Denmark, Hereward still posed a threat, albeit a minor one. Parallel to these events, both Edwin and Morcar fled the Norman court and would later on revolt again. There are no records that show the two brothers' interest in fighting alongside Hereward, but we do have records that Morcar met up with Hereward on the Isle of Ely and stayed there, possibly during the spring of 1071. William, who was back in England, was ready to squash the last rebellion that the two brothers would stage.

While fleeing William's forces and moving to Scotland, Edwin was betrayed by his own men and killed on the spot. In the meantime, the king issued an order to build a causeway around Ely, making a blockade by both land and sea. The subsequent siege of the isle lasted throughout the summer of 1071, with William once again utilizing his proven tactic of raiding the lands around the castle until he had fully intimidated the locals.

The monks of Ely soon sued for peace, and William entered the isle as a victor. Hereward was said to have escaped William, roaming the fens and fighting his resistance, but the veracity of this claim cannot be verified by historical records. Morcar surrendered and would remain a prisoner of both William and William's successors until he died, sometime after 1087.

Around this time, King William issued an order that all royal writs, i.e., formally issued orders, as well as writ-charters, would no longer be written in Old English but exclusively in Latin. William himself didn't speak Old English, though there are implications that he tried to do so but gave up soon after due to his advanced age and lifestyle, which prevented him from learning the language properly. And while he could have retained Old English as the language for royal writs since he had people in his court who understood both languages, his decision might have been both tactical and practical in nature. He most likely wanted to impose the Norman law quite literally on the local English subjects, but we can't neglect the fact that, save for rare exceptions, every single secular and religious noble in England was now a Norman, which would make issuing writs and writ-charters in Old English difficult.

Malcolm of Scotland and 1073

King Malcolm III of Scotland had been anything but a bit player during William's reign. For years, he provided sanctuary for the Norman king's opponents, making it extremely difficult for William and his close allies to maintain control of the kingdom. In addition, by the end of 1070, he married Margaret, the sister of Edgar Ætheling, all but publicly mocking William with this act. To add insult to injury, their children were all named after the English kings who came before William: Edward, Edmund, Æthelred, and Edgar. Not only was this a show of open support to the regime that wanted to overthrow William, but this was also an open declaration to the very throne of England. William would have to ride north again.

After the Harrying of the North, Malcolm freely raided the areas just south of his kingdom, taking many slaves. At the time, slavery was more or less the norm in Scotland, while in William's England, at least by the end of his reign, at least 10 percent of all people were slaves. William would impose a law that prevented the sale of slaves overseas, but there was still effectively no law against the practice itself. Moreover, aside from the Scots, the Welsh had a culture of enslaving their opponents. However, the Norman society was, overall, not slave-oriented, and as the years progressed, owning slaves in England had all but vanished by the 13th century.

William would begin his advance to conquer Scotland in 1072, quickly reaching the borders of Malcolm's kingdom and earning some military successes. The two men would eventually meet at Abernethy to discuss peace. This treaty stipulated that Malcolm submit to William as a vassal, which Malcolm did, and it might have even included two additional conditions: that Malcolm give up his son Duncan as a hostage and that Edgar Ætheling be driven out of the Scottish court. Although William didn't conquer Scotland and integrate it into his kingdom, his sovereignty over Malcolm proved that he definitely had the power and the capability to do so had he wanted. It was the year 1072, and already the world would have the first glimpses of what would become Great Britain.

Upon William's return to Normandy in early 1073, he had to deal with an uprising in Maine. Azzo d'Este had to leave Maine for unknown reasons, leaving it in the hands of Geoffrey of Mayenne and Gersendis, which sparked an affair between them. The citizens of Le Mans would rise up and eject them from the city at least two times, even asking Count Fulk IV to intervene, but the invaders kept coming back, and it seemed that nothing short of William's direct intervention would help.

William retook Maine surprisingly quickly after his return from England. By March 1073, he had taken Fresnay-sur-Sarthe (where Roger of Montgomery's son, Robert of Bellême, was knighted), then Sillé, and finally Le Mans itself. Once again, William successfully consolidated power in the region, and once again, he did so quickly and efficiently, using the same tactics of devastating the countryside and crushing the morale of his opponents. A mere month later, William's ally, Pope Alexander II, died, and Archdeacon Hildebrand succeeded him, taking the name of Gregory VII. As history would show, Pope Gregory would be another one of William's supporters, a further indicator that the king was still a force to be reckoned with.

Thwarting Edgar

After King Malcolm's loss against the Conqueror, Edgar Ætheling sought refuge in Flanders with William's opponent Robert the Frisian. In 1074, while William was spending the year in Normandy, Edgar returned to the Scottish court, and not long after, he received an order from King Philip I of France to turn against William once again. The French king offered Edgar some of his own lands and a castle near the border of Normandy, expecting the deposed English noble to attack William's homeland directly. Edgar embarked upon this mission, but a shipwreck would prevent his plans. Upon his return to Scotland, he received orders from King Malcolm to seek William in Normandy and submit to him. Setting off from Durham to Normandy, the noble of Wessex finally submitted completely to the Conqueror, which the latter accepted with great honors, allowing Edgar to live out his days in England with his own estates in Hertfordshire. True to his word, Edgar never rebelled again during William's reign, and after the king's death, he went to Italy for a brief period. Edgar would live a long and semi-eventful life, dying sometime around 1126.

Depiction of Edgar Ætheling from a roll chronicle depicting the English kings, circa 13th century
https://commons.wikimedia.org/wiki/File:Edgar_the_%C3%86theling.jpg

Revolt of the Earls

The year 1075 would prove to be just as eventful for William as the ones that preceded it. It was marked by possibly the last large-scale rebellion among the English, popularly known as the Revolt of the Earls. Though the whole affair took place in 1075, after the king had returned to England, the seeds for the rebellion had already been sown.

The earls who would rebel were all close to William in one way or another. The first and most prominent of these rebel leaders was Ralph of Guader, the Earl of East Anglia. Ralph inherited the post from his father, Ralph the Staller, a Breton aristocrat who had received the earldom after the Conquest. The second earl was Roger of Breteuil, the 2nd Earl of Hereford. His father was the late William Fitz Osbern, who had been one of William's closest allies. Roger's sister Emma would also play a prominent role in the revolt. The third and final earl was Waltheof, Earl of Northumbria, one of William's most treasured collaborators who seems to have been marginalized more and more as the years went on. In the early stages of the revolt, the belligerents sought help from the future Danish King Cnut, the son of Sweyn II (and whose fleet of 200 ships arrived too late to help the rebels), as well as some Welsh nobility due to Roger owning some lands there and his supposed good relations with the Welsh.

As for the main reason for the rebellion, nearly all medieval historians believe that the catalyst was Ralph's marriage to Emma. William might not have approved the marriage, or there could have been a misunderstanding, but whatever the case was, Ralph wasn't supposed to marry one of Fitz Osbern's children, which was a proposition the young earl of East Anglia just couldn't accept.

The revolt had issues from its earliest days. Waltheof would come clean about the rebel plans to Archbishop Lanfranc, possibly alluding that he had been coerced into doing it. Lanfranc would write to Roger several times, asking him to come to his senses, before excommunicating him entirely and letting William know what was going on. Lanfranc tried to negotiate peace without William even being there, which might appear rude and self-important on the surface, but if examined more closely, we can see that William put a great deal of trust in the archbishop of Canterbury, hence why he would tend to the matters of the state.

The whole revolt was effectively crushed by William's men in England. While rallying his troops to go east, Roger was intercepted at the river Severn, where he was struck by a united force under Bishop Wulfstan, which contained people such as Walter of Lacy, Abbot Æthelwig of Evesham, and Urse d'Abetot. A considerably larger army, led by Odo of Bayeux, Bishop Geoffrey of Coutances, Richard Fitz Gilbert, and William of Warenne, beat Ralph near Cambridge in the battle at Fawdon in

Whaddon. Ralph first fled to Norwich, where he left his new wife Emma behind to hold the position, while he went to the Danish to seek support (and later came back when the aforementioned 200 ships sailed for the island). Bishop Geoffrey and William of Warenne, alongside a noble named Robert Malet, would then besiege Emma's castle for a few months until she agreed to surrender, provided her men were spared. Everyone in her service was deprived of their property and lands, but they were given forty days to leave the island. Both Emma and Ralph left England and settled in Brittany, though not at the same time. The last eventful string of events to happen was the Danish arrival in the northeast of England and their raids in and around York. Once again, they arrived at the very end of the rebellion, and once again, they were ill-equipped to fight William's forces. It didn't help that William had finally caught wind of what was going on and sailed back to England at some point in 1075. Cnut and his forces retreated, not wanting to risk a battle with the English king.

William treated the rebels monstrously. Roger was imprisoned for life, and he was released only briefly after William's death, after which he was promptly beheaded. The king's soldiers were ordered to mutilate the rebels, with the most common method involving the lopping off of their right feet. Waltheof didn't go unpunished either. He would be beheaded in 1076, making him the first Englishman to lose his life in such a gruesome way on the island. Because of his disposition and actions, Waltheof was regarded as a bit of a martyr.

1076 to 1078 on the Continent

Not long after his arrival in Brittany, Count Ralph would seize control of Dol, an important castle, which prompted William to besiege it. Ralph had the backing of the French King Philip, who had been at odds with William for years now. In the ensuing Battle of Dol, he would deal William his first proper defeat in battle, forcing the siege to be lifted. The shift in power dynamics didn't change much; however, a subsequent attack on Maine by the forces of Fulk IV of Anjou, sometime between 1076 and 1077, would eventually end with the count being wounded and William taking the win, allowing him to consolidate the region once again. At around the same time, the Count of Amiens, Simon of Crépy, retired to a monastery, bestowing the region of Vexin to King Philip. Simon had been one of William's supporters on the continent, and handing Vexin, a buffer border region that stood between France and Normandy, was a dangerous move on his part. William had to negotiate peace on two fronts, first with King Philip at some point in 1077 and then with Count Fulk the following year.

In his fifties, William was still a force to be reckoned with, but the events that took place during these years were definitely an indicator that he was starting to lose his edge. This was also reflected in his appearance, considering he had, at that point, gained a lot of weight and lost most of the physical luster that made him stand out twenty or even ten years before. His overseas empire was more or less stable, but as an elderly monarch, he found himself in the same situation his own entourage was in all those years back, a situation where the new generation was dissatisfied with their predecessors. And in medieval times, those inter-generational quarrels could only end with violence.

Robert's Rebellion

Robert, later to be known as Curthose ("short stockings"), was William's heir apparent and his eldest son. As early as his tender years, his name had appeared on charters next to both William's and Matilda's, showing just how much care the couple put into making Robert "heir material" from the very beginning. However, the young noble might have felt sidelined, much like Waltheof back in England. Some sources claim that William refused to give control of Normandy and Maine to Robert.

In terms of succession or even appointing co-regents, this act wouldn't be a problem since Robert was already in his early twenties, way past the age when medieval monarchs were usually crowned. If William had indeed refused to give control of these territories to Robert, the reasons that governed that decision are left to speculation.

Sometime between 1077 and 1078, Robert left Normandy with several nobles, such as Robert of Bellême, William of Breteuil, and Roger. All of these men were sons of William's supporters: Roger's father was Richard Fitz Gilbert, Breteuil's was the late Fitz Osbern, and Robert was the son of Roger of Montgomery. The three men chose Rémalard Castle as their base, raiding Normandy once they settled there. William managed to drive them off, but the rebels simply settled in a new castle called Gerberoi (also spelled Gerberoy), which was provided by King Philip. Young Robert's forces were growing in number, which was especially dangerous for Normandy, considering that so many of William's direct opponents supported his rebellious son. In January 1079, William besieged the castle, but the rebels actually managed to deploy a military unit and catch the English king by surprise. Stories suggest that Robert had even unhorsed William and that the only reason why the king survived was thanks to a certain English soldier called Toki, son of Wigod. Toki supposedly gave his life for the king, allowing him to retreat. The siege was lifted, leaving Robert and his men unbeaten.

The gravity of this loss and humiliation didn't elude William. However, the fact that it had been his own son complicated matters, so the two had to reach some sort of agreement. By April 12th, 1080, the two had reconciled, with Robert once again being reinstated as the heir apparent of Normandy. In addition, William would take him during his trips across the country and even across the Channel. Nevertheless, the relationship between father and son remained strained at best.

The Scots and the Welsh in the Early 1080s

Back in Britain, news of William's defeat at Gerberoi was everywhere, and at some point, it had reached the ears of King Malcolm of Scotland. As early as September 1079, the Scots raided the territory south of the Tweed River. The month-long raid wasn't properly dealt with by the Normans in charge of Northumbria, in particular, by the earl of the region William Walcher. The locals would rebel against Walcher and kill him on May 14th of the same year, prompting a response from William.

With Odo of Bayeux handling the rebels, William and his son crossed the Channel in July. Several months later, Robert would be given orders to raid Scotland, which he did, entering Lothian and forcing Malcolm to sue for peace. Once again, William proved to be the dominant force on the island, and the sacking of Lothian had, alongside his success at Gerberoi, demonstrated that Robert was an effective warrior on either side of the Channel.

Between 1080 and 1081, William was in England, where he entertained the papal embassy and refused their request to do fealty to Rome in the name of England. During this time, he also visited Wales, more than likely to use the political situation there to his advantage. He didn't conquer Wales, but the mere fact that he could impose his will on the Welsh proves that William had, indeed, been the proper overlord of Britain, by far the first king to do so.

The decade had been an eventful one for William. He had consolidated power in ways few other rulers could at the time, all while maintaining his piety and making sure peace was nurtured, even if his means of obtaining that peace were less than wholesome, to say the least. And while the losses he suffered by the end of the 1070s were a clear sign that he was past his prime, the final years still had a few surprises for the first Norman king of England. More importantly, he had a few surprises of his own.

A statue depicting Malcolm III, King of Scots, Scottish National Portrait Gallery
Stephencdickson, CC BY-SA 4.0 <https://creativecommons.org/licenses/by-sa/4.0>, via Wikimedia Commons https://commons.wikimedia.org/wiki/File:Statue_of_King_Malcolm_III,_Scottish_National_Portrait_Gallery.jpg

Chapter 4 – Final Years and Death

The year 1082 saw William arresting and imprisoning his own halfbrother Odo of Bayeux. The precise reasons for this arrest are not known, and while it is tempting to think that William was pressured into arresting Odo due to his shady dealings with his earldom and the Church in the 1070s (including some land inconsistencies Odo had inherited all the way from the regime of Harold Godwinson and the nobles who held the land back then), that is not directly stated by any reliable records from that era. We do know that Odo planned on going to southern Italy, but whether he wanted to invade it with William's vassals as his troops (an act that would infuriate William, as nobles had no right to recruit militants without the king's expressed consent) or simply planned on going there to take the title of pope isn't known to us. Odo would remain imprisoned for years, only being released shortly before William's death.

Matters didn't seem to get any better for William the next year either. His son Robert staged another rebellion, and trouble in Maine was also brewing, resulting in a rebellion in 1084 by a noble named Hubert of

Beaumont-au-Maine. But none of these events would affect William as much as what happened to his queen. After a possible long-term illness, Matilda, Queen of England and wife of William the Conqueror, passed away on November 2nd, 1083. William would never recover from this loss.

Most of the problems that followed seemed to pass swiftly. Herbert would take refuge at the castle at Sainte-Suzanne during the rebellion, which William would besiege for two years, finally beating the rebel. As he was prone to do, William granted Herbert a pardon and restored him to power. In the meantime, the king was preparing for a possible Danish invasion, headed by their king, Cnut IV. However, Cnut died in July of 1086, thwarting those plans, though both sides were eagerly waiting for the battle to come. Nevertheless, one particular event does stand out, and had it not been for William's Conquest in 1066, it would have been the event that made William go down in history.

During Christmas of 1085, William commissioned a lengthy text that contained a survey of all the land properties that both he and his supporters held across England. Though it was incomplete and contains some questionable parts, this survey is incredibly thorough. It mentions all of the counties, lists the holdings of each owner before the Conquest, what the value of the property was, what its tax assessment was, and the number of resources the owner had available (peasants, plows, livestock, tools, etc.). The document, which saw the light of day by August of the following year, was officially named the Domesday Book, and to modern historians, it's an invaluable source of English life during William's reign.

William's final year would see him go out with flair. After leaving England by the end of 1086 and arriving in northern France, he arranged for his daughter Constance to marry Alan, the Duke of Brittany. While he was still waging wars against the French, who were allied with his son Robert in another rebellion, the king started to invade Vexin, then under

French control, in July. The siege of Mantes would prove to be William's last, as he fell ill and was taken to Rouen to the priory of Saint Gervase. Before his death, he settled the matter of bequests. It would be William's final wish that Robert Curthose succeed him in Normandy, with his second son, William, continuing as the king in England. Henry, the youngest son, didn't receive any territory, but like numerous priests and churchgoers, he received a financial inheritance. Supposedly, William also ordered that money be distributed to the poor. Finally, all of his prisoners, including his half-brother Odo, were to be released.

On September 9th, 1087, William the Conqueror, Duke of Normandy and King of England, the most powerful man of northern France and the progenitor of a cross-Channel empire that would come to affect the world in numerous ways, died at Rouen at the age of fifty-nine.

Chapter 5 – William's Character: Personality Traits, Virtues, Flaws, and Motivations

Discerning the character of a medieval monarch is an impossible task. Written sources from the period of a king's reign usually tend to fall under one of two camps. They are either openly antagonistic or apologetic to an absurd degree. Most of the writers who composed works of history in both ancient and medieval times had no sense of objective criticism, nor did they behave as dispassionate, non-partisan actors. Most likely, they would write about events with exaggeration, open omission of facts, and add made-up or incorrect factoids due to a lack of information. With that in mind, we must take everything written about William's character with a grain of salt. However, by focusing on his actions, a somewhat clear picture of the Conqueror does present itself.

William was, even for his time, a cunning tactician. He was a man who could read the situation around him well, allowing him to prepare for an attack or an action in advance and almost always succeeding on the battlefield. By the time he entered his forties, the Conqueror had become the king of England, still ruled as the duke of Normandy (which had been greatly expanded and consolidated under his rule), and a sovereign of at least several different vassal lands, which were independent in name only. Aside from reading the situation, he was also an expert in distributing his troops, as well as treating them appropriately after a military success. But what isn't often discussed is William's ability to have a proper psychological impact on his opponents. Ravaging the lands before the attack, building castles at strategic places, taking the crown and wearing it in a recently destroyed city—all of these actions came from someone who knew how to instill fear into his adversaries.

Due to the number of churches he built or granted gifts to, we can also safely assume that William was a pious man. While there definitely was political expediency to having the Church on your side (which necessitated gifts and grants), the king was more than likely genuine about his faith in God, often seeking guidance from priests on various subject matters, irrespective of how he might have treated other members of the clergy.

Naturally, we can't forget William's cruelty, specifically the horrors of the Harrying of the North and other massacres. Without a doubt, William was a ruthless, brutal ruler who knew how to use violence and use it well. At certain times, genuine anger manifested into these actions, such as when his mother's family was mocked at Alençon or when he lost the battle against his eldest son. But anger was not the common element of his ruthlessness, as it was clearly tactical and applied when the need for it arose.

Though William might have been a prudent fighter, he would, at times, be an impatient ruler. Oftentimes when presented with a dilemma, he would simply decide in the favor of one of the belligerents as quickly as possible. His decision to rule in favor of Marmoutier Abbey during its dispute with Saint-Pierre de la Couture Abbey of Le Mans was one such example of this behavior.

One detail does set William apart from other medieval rulers. Unlike the vast majority of kings, dukes, princes, counts, despots, and emperors, William did not seem to have a mistress. This can be attributed to his childhood and his willingness to abstain from sex due to his strong religious feelings influenced by his father's reign, but there could be a different reason, one that isn't often found with the rulers of the time. Namely, William might have genuinely been in love with Matilda, having included her in a great number of his business affairs and spending as much time as he could with her. Matilda's death left him genuinely devastated, as did the death of their son many years before, suggesting that the bond between the two had been strong. Despite his harsh dealings with his enemies and the atrocities he committed, William definitely had a soft, gentle side to him, a side that was surely best known by Matilda (and perhaps Matilda alone).

In terms of what drove William to do what he did, there are several different answers. First and foremost, it could have been just a genuine lust for power. Since his late adolescence, William had been winning one battle after another, with eerie efficiency. And the more his dukedom and later his kingdom grew, the more he must have felt entitled to all that power. But even if that were the case, we can't neglect his early years, when his conquest was merely one of consolidation and maintaining the status quo. As much as William might have enjoyed taking over new lands, his primary concern had always been to rule over a stable realm. He would do anything, from freeing and pardoning his old enemies to putting both the guilty and the innocent to the sword, just to achieve that goal. And while nothing can excuse the war atrocities that William's regime brought upon both northern France and England, we also can't deny his proactive thinking and his willingness to go the distance when it came to running his realm.

William's dominions around 1087, from the Historical Atlas by William R. Shepherd, 1926
https://commons.wikimedia.org/wiki/File:Williams_dominions_1087.jpg

Conclusion

As stated, the entirety of facts that comprise William's fascinating life is too much for the scope of this book. Whether it was his love of a good hunt or the numerous churches he built and gifted over the years, whether it was the friends he made along the way or the surprising enemies that cropped up out of nowhere, it's incredibly difficult to summarize. So, one question does remain—what kind of legacy did William the Conqueror leave?

The first, most obvious impact William made on the world was how the Conquest completely changed the entire social, political, religious, and even ethnic makeup of an entire nation. He was far from being the first one to unite all of the Anglo-Saxons, but with the implementation of Norman rule, he would be the progenitor of homogenizing the land, with the descendants of both Anglo-Saxons and Normans creating an entirely new identity, that of the English, which still stands strong today.

Next, there's the Conquest itself. Even though he wasn't necessarily thought of as a bastard during his time, William would have still been a duke from a comparatively small duchy. Yet somehow, he managed to create a cross-Channel empire by crushing enemy after enemy with patience and ruthless efficiency. He showed the medieval world that anything could be possible, even taking over a kingdom that he technically had nothing to do with.

And speaking of his new kingdom, the Norman monarch let the world know that maintaining an empire of that size, along with the geographical and hydrographical difficulties that came with it, might have been difficult, but it was definitely possible. All it took was choosing the right people for the job and either punishing or pardoning those who would undermine it.

But William's story is fascinating in other ways too. He is the living proof that not everything has to be done by the norm, especially when it comes to aristocratic marriages. With zero illegitimate children and only a single marriage to his name, the duke of Normandy and king of England proved that true love is possible, even during an age that most people mislabel as the Dark Ages. His care and devotion to Matilda and enormous sadness over her death show us that William, as powerful of a Conqueror as he might have been, was still a human being, one who's complicated and not easily picked apart.

Sadly, William's cross-Channel empire would not last, as his sons and their supporters would tear it apart in a mere few generations. His own grave would be desecrated several times throughout history. But William's story still lives on. He would forever be remembered as the last foreign power to have invaded England and conquered it, as well as the first man to hold dominion, directly or indirectly, over all of Britain. Few rulers in history would achieve what William the Conqueror had, and for better or for worse, he shall remain the single most important turning point and arguably the single most important individual in all of British history.

Here's another book by Captivating History that you might like

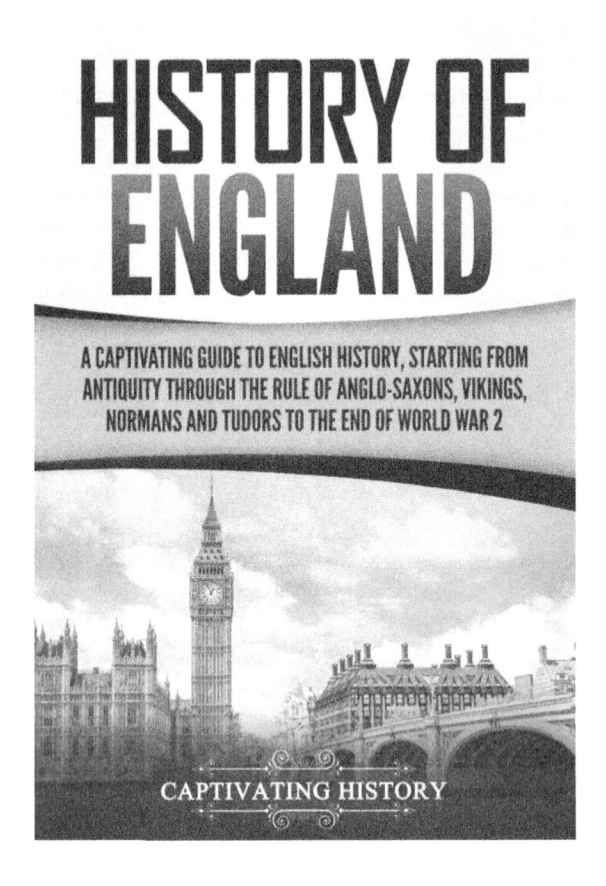

HISTORY OF ENGLAND

A CAPTIVATING GUIDE TO ENGLISH HISTORY, STARTING FROM ANTIQUITY THROUGH THE RULE OF ANGLO-SAXONS, VIKINGS, NORMANS AND TUDORS TO THE END OF WORLD WAR 2

CAPTIVATING HISTORY

Free Bonus from Captivating History (Available for a Limited time)

Hi History Lovers!

Now you have a chance to join our exclusive history list so you can get your first history ebook for free as well as discounts and a potential to get more history books for free! Simply visit the link below to join.

Captivatinghistory.com/ebook

Also, make sure to follow us on Facebook, Twitter and Youtube by searching for Captivating History.

Bibliography

10 Facts about the Battle of Hastings, Sally Coffey, 2019, The Official Magazine Britain, Chelsea Magazine Co, www.britain-magazine.com/

1066 and the Norman Conquest, English Heritage, 2019, www.english-heritage.org.uk/

1066: A Timeline of the Norman Conquest, Peter Konieczny, October 8, 2017, Medieval Warfare, Karwansaray Publishers, www.karwansaraypublishers.com.

A History of the Norman Conquest of 1066, Robert Wilde, April 7, 2017, Thought Co., www.thoughtco.com

Alfred the Great (849 AD – 899 AD), BBC: History, http://www.bbc.co.uk/history.

Alfred: King of Wessex, Dorothy Whitelock, Encyclopedia Britannica, last edited January 1, 2019, www.britannica.com.

Anglo-Saxon Chronical, Editors of Encyclopedia Britannica, 2019, www.britannica.com

Before the Norman Conquest, A History of the County of York: The City of York, ed. P M Tillott (London, 1961), pp. 2-24. British History Online www.british-history.ac.uk/ 4 October 2019.

Harold Godwinson, Mark Cartwright, January 14, 2019, Ancient History Encyclopedia, www.ancient.eu

Harold II (Godwineson) (c.1020 – 1066), 2014, BBC, www.bbc.co.uk/history

History: Norman Britain, Neil McIntosh, November 6, 2014, BBC, www.bbc.co.uk/history.

Overview: The Vikings, 800 to 1066, Professor Edward James, March 29, 2011, History, BBC, www.bbc.co.uk/history.

Robert I, Duke of Normandy, Editors of Britannica, 2019, www.britannica.com

The Art of Conquest in England and Normandy, Dr. Diane Reilly, October 4, 2019, Khan Academy, www.khanacademy.org.

The Battle of Hastings, Return to Anglo-Saxon England, 2019, penelope.uchicago.edu/

The Bayeux Tapestry, Dr. Kristine Tanton, October 4, 2019, Khan Academy, www.khanacademy.org.

The Domesday Book, Ben Johnson, 2019, Historic UK, www.historic-uk.com/

The History Files :Part 1: Western Decline, Peter Kessler, June 30, 2007, The History Files, Kessler Associates, www.historyfiles.co.uk/.

The Impact of the Norman Conquest of England, Mark Cartwright, January 23, 2019, Ancient History Encyclopedia, www.ancient.eu/.

The Incredible Life of Harald Hardrada: The Last of the 'Great Vikings, Dattaterya Mandal, September 5, 2015, Realm of History, www.realmofhistory.com/

The Norman Invasion of 1066 CE, Western Civilization, October 4, 2019, OER Services, courses.lumenlearning.com.

The Roman 'Brexit': how life in Britain Changed after 409AD, Will Bowden, 2019, University of Nottingham, The Conversation US Inc, theconversation.com.

The Romans in England, Ben Johnson, 2019, Historic UK Ltd, www.historic-uk.com/.

William I 'The Conqueror' (r.1066-1087), 2019, The Royal Household, Crown, www.royal.uk/william-the-conqueror

Bachrach, B.S. (1985): "On the Origins of William the Conqueror's Horse Transports," In *Technology and Culture* Vol. 26, No. 3, (pp. 505-531). Baltimore, MD, USA: The Johns Hopkins University Press and Society for the History of Technology.

Bates, D. (2016): *William the Conqueror.* New Haven, CT, USA: Yale University Press.

Brooke, Z. N. (1911): "Pope Gregory VII's Demand for Fealty from William the Conqueror," In *The English Historical Review* Vol. 26, No. 102, (pp. 225-238). Oxford, UK: Oxford University Press.

Clanchy, M. T. (2014): *England and Its Rulers 1066-1307.* Hoboken, NJ, USA: Wiley-Blackwell.

Clarke, G. (1895): "Are We All Descendants of the Conqueror," In *The North American Review* Vol. 160, No. 458, (pp. 117-118). Cedar Falls, IA, USA:

University of Northern Iowa.

Douglas, D. C. (1999): *William the Conqueror.* New Haven, CT, USA & London, UK: Yale University Press.

Douglas, D. C. (1927): "A Charter of Enfeoffment under William the Conqueror," In *The English Historical Review* Vol. 42, No. 166, (pp. 245-247). Oxford, UK: Oxford University Press.

Encyclopedia Britannica (1981), Retrieved on November 5th 2020, from https://www.britannica.com.

Gomme, E. E. C (1909): *The Anglo-Saxon Chronicle, Newly Translated by E. E. C. Gomme, B.A.* London, UK: George Bell and Sons.

Haskins, C. H. (1908): "The Norman 'Consuetudines et Iusticie'of William the Conqueror," In *The English Historical Review* Vol. 23, No. 91, (pp. 502-508). Oxford, UK: Oxford University Press.

Haskins, C. H. (1909): "Normandy under William the Conqueror," In *The American Historical Review* Vol. 14, No. 3, (pp. 453-476). Oxford, UK: Oxford University Press on behalf of the American Historical Association.

Higham, N. J. (2015): *The Anglo-Saxon World.* New Haven, Ct, USA & London, UK: Yale University Press

Hudson, B. (1994): "William the Conqueror and Ireland," In *Irish Historical Studies* Vol. 29, No. 114, (pp. 145-158). Dublin, Ireland: Irish Historical Studies Publications Ltd.

Lennard, R. (1945): "The Destruction of Woodland in the Eastern Counties under William the Conqueror," In *The Economic History Review* Vol. 15, No. 1/2, (pp. 36-43). Hoboken, NJ, USA: Wiley-Blackwell on behalf of the Economic History Society.

Medieval Chronicles™ (2014). Retrieved on November 5th 2020, from http://www.medievalchronicles.com.

Moore, J.R. (1951): "Windsor Forest and William III," In *Modern Language Notes* Vol. 66, No. 7, (pp. 451-454). Baltimore, MD, USA: The Johns Hopkins University Press.

Round, J. H. and Stevenson, W. H. (1897): "An Old English Charter of William the Conqueror, 1068 (?)," In *The English Historical Review* Vol. 12, No. 45, (pp. 105-110). Oxford, UK: Oxford University Press.

van Houts, E. M. C. (1986): "The Origins of Herleva, Mother of William the Conqueror," In *The English Historical Review* Vol. 101, No. 399, (pp. 399-404). Oxford, UK: Oxford University Press.

Wikipedia (January 15, 2001), Retrieved on November 5th 2020, from https://www.wikipedia.org/.

Printed in Great Britain
by Amazon